# 30 DAYS
# OF REFLECTION FROM A
# SURRENDERED HEART

# 30 DAYS OF REFLECTION FROM A SURRENDERED HEART

Reflection, devotion, and guide
to inspire and awaken
the soul and spirit.

**TAMARA SCOTT**

PCB

Published by Purple Chair Books and Educational Products, LLC

First Printing, 2025

Copyright © Tamara L. Scott, 2025

Scott, Tamara 1988-

30 Days of Reflection from a Surrendered Heart

By Tamara L. Scott

ISBN: 978-1-953671-07-3

Christian Life/ Spiritual 1. Title Printed in the United States of America

Interior designed by Md Al Amin

Cover designed by Sadia A@Sadia_Coverz

# FOREWARD

In the embrace of quiet mornings, with the gentle light of dawn filtering through the windows, I have often found the author deep in prayer and reflection. Her journey of faith, filled with grace, strength, and unwavering devotion, has been a beacon of light to me and to all who are blessed to know her. With profound admiration and joy, I write this foreword for her spiritual reflection and devotion book, *30 Days of Reflection from a Surrendered Heart*.

Over the years, I have witnessed her navigate the intricacies of life with a heart fully surrendered to the will of God. Her reflections, born out of personal trials, triumphs, and a deep-seated love for the Lord, are a testament to her faith. This book is a collection of those reflections—a journey into the heart of a woman who has found solace, strength, and purpose in her walk with God.

This book is more than just a collection of thoughts; it is a labor of love—a testament to the author's deep concern for those seeking a little nudge or spiritual guidance. It offers profound insights, wisdom, and reminders from a heart devoted to a God who loves, is compassionate, and has the power to heal, redeem, and save anyone.

Each day within these pages offers a unique glimpse into the soul of a surrendered heart. Tamara shares her intimate conversations with God, the wisdom gleaned from Scripture, the beauty of God's creation, and the lessons learned from life's experiences. Her words are a soothing balm for the weary soul and a guiding light for those seeking a deeper connection with the Divine.

In *30 Days of Reflection from a Surrendered Heart*, you will find a companion for your spiritual journey. Whether you are seeking peace in turbulent times, strength in moments of weakness, or a closer walk with God, Tamara's reflections will inspire, challenge, and uplift you. She invites you to join her in this sacred space, where the heart is bare before God, and His love and grace abound.

As you embark on this 30-day journey, may you find the same peace and joy Tamara has found in surrendering to God's will. May her reflections draw you closer to God's heart and inspire you to live a life of faith, love, and surrender.

With heartfelt love and gratitude,

*Dr. David Scott, Ed.D. D.Min.*
*Pastor, Bible Teacher, Theologian,*
*Author of* The Unchanging Truth: Jesus Still the Way, The Truth & Life

# ACKNOWLEDGEMENTS

I want to begin by giving all honor and glory to God. I have completed this journey through His grace, strength, and unfailing love. His guidance and presence in my life have been my constant source of encouragement and peace. I am eternally grateful for His purpose and the faith to walk in it.

Thank you to my loving husband. Your unwavering support, love, and patience have been more than I ever hoped or asked for. You have stood by me through every challenge, offering wisdom and encouragement. Thank you for being my rock, confidante, and greatest cheerleader. I could not have accomplished this without your constant belief in me.

To my sister/cousin, Juana, I want to celebrate your unwavering consistency and remarkable growth in the Lord. Your faith journey is inspiring, and your dedication is a powerful testament to the Lord's faithfulness. Thank you for your steadfast support, for loving me unconditionally, and for inviting God to work in your life.

To my beloved Sister-in-Christ, Shona, your prayers, encouragement, and spiritual guidance have been a blessing. Thank you for illuminating God's promises and journeying with me in faith. Your friendship and sisterhood beautifully embody God's love in my life.

To my sister-in-Christ, Mellonease, your continuous prayers and uplifting spirit inspire me greatly. Your kindness and love empower me and serve as a profound source of strength. You have been a blessing this season, and I am deeply grateful for your unwavering support.

Finally, I thank all those who have prayed for me and offered support along the way. This accomplishment is a testimony to the power of faith, love, and community.

Before confronting the day's demands and challenges, there is no better decision than to seek the face of Elohim, the God of the universe and all creation.

# TABLE OF CONTENTS

Foreword ..................................................................................... I

Acknowledgements .................................................................. III

Introduction ................................................................................ 1

**DAYR 1.** Do you know the God you worship? ........................ 3
**DAYR 2.** God's Word is our lifeline ......................................... 9
**DAYR 3.** Intentionality ............................................................ 15
**DAYR 4.** True Wealth ............................................................. 20
**DAYR 5.** The Narrow Gate .................................................... 25
**DAYR 6.** Keep God Involved in Everything! ........................ 31
**DAYR 7.** Prayer ...................................................................... 38
**DAYR 8.** Closeted Christians ................................................ 43
**DAYR 9.** A Daily Walk .......................................................... 49
**DAYR 10.** Validation .............................................................. 53
**DAYR 11.** Sometimes Families Don't Understand ............... 58
**DAYR 12.** Make Jesus a Daily Choice! ................................. 63
**DAYR 13.** Don't be Deceived ................................................. 68
**DAYR 14.** The Pursuit of Holiness ........................................ 73
**DAYR 15.** The Favor of the Lord ........................................... 78
**DAYR 16.** Preach, Teach, or Reach! ...................................... 82
**DAYR 17.** Spiritual Laziness .................................................. 87
**DAYR 18.** The Uneasy Path ................................................... 92
**DAYR 19.** Drifting Away ........................................................ 97
**DAYR 20.** Children Derailed ................................................ 102

DAYR 21. A Time for Reflection........................................................................108
DAYR 22. The Ups, Downs, and Flow of Life.................................................113
DAYR 23. Essential to the Faith Journey: Relationship with God .........118
DAYR 24. God in Uncertain Times..................................................................124
DAYR 25. The Struggle and Battle of Being a Christian............................129
DAYR 26. More of Jesus and Less of the World............................................134
DAYR 27. Life Can Be Tough!...........................................................................139
DAYR 28. Rejoice. Believers Will Never Die! ...............................................146
DAYR 29. Highlight the Goodness of God ....................................................151
DAYR 30. Willing, Waiting, and Available.....................................................156

# INTRODUCTION

I never expected to find myself on the exciting journey of writing a book! I never thought I'd have enough to share or anything meaningful for others. But life has a way of surprising us. We can never really know how God might use us if we're open, patient, and ready to embrace what comes our way. We each have a unique plan and purpose in God's heart that goes far beyond what we might imagine. The words in this book reflect the love, devotion, and joy of a heart that has been changed and inspired by a caring and compassionate God. I'm thrilled to share this journey with you!

Reflecting on my life, I recognize that God has intricately woven His plan into my journey for quite some time. He began this remarkable work by igniting a longing in my heart to rise earlier each morning and dedicate intentional, planned time to be with Him. This routine, born from a desire to grow closer to Him, has led to significant growth in my faith. In the quiet hours, before the world awakens, I find the perfect setting to sit in His presence and wait. During these sacred moments, free from distractions, He communicates with me through His Word.

As I developed a daily morning prayer and Bible study routine, God revealed amazing insights to me. Over time, He encouraged me to share these revelations with others. Despite my doubts and fears, I obediently began to share what He impressed upon my heart and soul. To my surprise, my sharing has blessed, inspired, and encouraged many people.

I never considered sharing my faith, beliefs, thoughts, or spiritual journey with others. However, over time, sharing became a common practice for me. Initially, I wanted to keep the insights God revealed to me through prayer, meditation, and His Word to myself. Yet, as the older generation used to say, "I couldn't keep it to myself." I never planned to do much more than occasionally post a few thoughts on social media, but as often happens, God had other plans for me.

I initially intended to share only brief snippets about God's love, compassion, grace, and mercy. However, my posts consistently evolved into longer and more detailed presentations. My expressions transformed from quick, short lines into much more heartfelt messages. The more time I spent with God, the more inspired I felt to share my thoughts. As Scripture states in John 7:38, "Whoever believes in me, as Scripture has said, rivers of living water will flow from within them."

This book powerfully reflects a heart transformed by the living God and celebrates the beauty of His unparalleled Word. Although writing a book was not my original intention, I am grateful for the opportunity to glorify God and inspire others to grow closer to Him. With the successful completion of this work, I firmly believe that God is pleased, His will is unfolding, and at least one soul will be drawn into His marvelous and eternal kingdom. To God be all the glory!

# DAY 1
# DO YOU KNOW THE GOD YOU WORSHIP?

**Colossians** 3:1-3 – "Since you have been raised to new life with Christ, set your sights on the realities of heaven, where Christ sits in the place of honor at God's right hand. Think about the things of heaven, not the things of the earth. For you have died to this life, and your real life is hidden with Christ in God."

Understanding our identity, especially our identity in Christ, is incredibly important. Proverbs 9:10 states, *"The fear of the Lord is the beginning of wisdom, and the knowledge of the Holy One is understanding."* Therefore, knowing and understanding who you serve and what it means to be a child of God is essential. Choosing to follow Christ, you embark on a transformative and spiritual awakening as you learn and grow. In the walk with Christ, we learn to take comfort in the words of Romans 8:37, *"In all these things we are more than conquerors through him who loved us."* From these words, we must acknowledge that God's promises are meant for believers who deliberately and intentionally placed their hope in Him.

People sometimes confuse their identities with roles, titles, and positions. However, our identity is revealed through our relationship with Christ Jesus. When the Holy Spirit enters our hearts, we become children of the Almighty God. His Spirit replaces the old character, nature, dwelling within us. With Christ living in us, He becomes the head of our lives, and we learn to surrender to Him fully. The Spirit of Christ guides and leads us in obedience. As our teacher, the Holy Spirit helps us apply the Word of God to our lives and navigates our journey toward complete sanctification. This transformation is a source of hope and inspiration, reminding us of the incredible power of God's love and grace.

Following Christ and being called His very own assures us that our Lord will never abandon us. Inspired by Christ's example in the Garden of Gethsemane, we must learn to completely surrender to God's plan for our lives, regardless of personal costs or challenges, emulating Christ's words: "Lord, not my will, but Your will be done." Dr. Luke recounts the Savior's agony in the garden, where Jesus's sweat fell like drops of blood, yet He fully submitted to the Father's will, saving humanity through His obedience. We must aspire to be like Christ, as Matthew 10:24-25 reminds us, *"Students are not greater than their teacher, and slaves are not greater than their master. Students should be like their teachers, and slaves like their masters."*

Our Savior, Jesus, understands our emotions, challenges, and struggles. In Hebrews 2:16-18, the author explains that the Son did not come to assist angels but to help the descendants of Abraham. Jesus had to be made like us to serve as our merciful and faithful High Priest before God. By becoming human in every way, yet without sin, He was able to offer a permanent and effective sacrifice to remove the sins of the people. Because He has suffered and been tested, Jesus can support us during our trials. Since He became human like us, He can show empathy and compassion toward us. He is more than willing and able to see beyond our every fault, frailty, and weakness and attends to all our needs.

Jesus, our faithful and compassionate High Priest, is our refuge during life's most significant trials and difficulties. He is always present to support us through the hurts and pain that sometimes overwhelms us. His grace and mercy are beyond comprehension, and His love is unconditional. We do not choose God; He chooses us. He sacrificed Himself on Calvary's cross so that we could experience a more abundant life now and in eternity. This abundance exceeds far beyond mere material possessions. Through His blood, Jesus purchased our right to the gift of eternal life.

The writer of 2 Corinthians 5:16 17 reminds us, "At one time we thought of Christ merely from a human point of view. How differently we know Him now! This means that anyone who belongs to Christ has become a new person. The old life is gone; a new life has begun!" Because of this transformation, we cannot continue living as before, for the Holy One now lives within us.

As children of God, we are called salt and light in a dark world, always mindful of our conduct, actions, and speech. As God's representatives, we are expected to emulate Him. Because we are His children, He has empowered us to achieve what may seem impossible. The scripture reminds us in Colossians 3:17: "Whatever you do or say, do it as a representative of the Lord Jesus, giving thanks through Him to God the Father." We are called to be living epistles. Through His Spirit, we can live according to His will. By His power, we can accomplish far more than we could have imagined, looking more and more like Him every day.

The Lord Jesus came to save the lost, and we are called to share this message and the good news with others. As followers of Christ, we have received the command of the Great Commission, which is recorded in Matthew 28:19-20: "Go and make disciples of all nations, baptizing them in the name of the Father and the Son and the Holy Spirit. Teach these new disciples to obey all the commands I have given you." It is God's will for us to win souls and bring them into the Kingdom, just as branches of a grand and majestic tree are expected to bear good fruit.

The Father is a skilled gardener, as described in John 15:1-3; Jesus says, "I am the true vine, and my Father is the gardener." He removes unfruitful branches and prunes those that bear fruit, aiming for greater productivity. God desires us to stand apart from the lost world, reaching out to the hurting and inviting all people from diverse backgrounds to come to Him.

# Prayer:

If you haven't accepted Christ yet, I pray that you make Him your Lord and Savior. If you have already given your life to Christ Jesus, I pray that you continue to follow and obey Him, live a righteous and holy life, and share the wonderful things He has done for you with the world. May you thrive, prosper, and grow in Christ, bearing fruit every season. In Jesus' Name, Amen!

# Meditating Scriptures:

**Colossians** 3: 16-17 – "Let the message about Christ, in all its richness, fill your lives. Teach and counsel each other with all the wisdom he gives. Sing psalms and hymns and spiritual songs to God with a thankful heart. And whatever you do or say, do it as a representative of the Lord Jesus, giving thanks to God the Father through him."

## Key Points and Reminders

- Your identity lies in Christ
- Emulate Christ by fully embracing obedience and surrender
- Allow Christ to dwell in your heart and mind

## Reflection

Life doesn't follow a straight path, even with strategic and detailed plans. Instead, it takes unexpected twists and turns, with starts and stops and unforeseen delays. However, regardless of the direction, the time it takes to reach our destination, or the challenges we face, our God, EL-GIBHOR (The Mighty God), is with us.

# DAY 2
# GOD'S WORD IS OUR LIFELINE

**Hebrews 4:12-13:** "For the word of God is living, effective, and sharper than any double-edged sword, penetrating the separation of soul and spirit, joints, and marrow. It can judge the thoughts and intentions of the heart. No creature is hidden from him, but all things are naked and exposed to the eyes of him to whom we must give an account."

Many people view the Bible as merely a book or a collection of laws designed to control their lives and make them unhappy. However, those with such views often have not read or studied the scriptures and rely on others' assumptions, speculations, or inaccurate comments. Unfortunately, most individuals have not read or studied the scriptures deeply enough to understand their meaning or to appreciate the cultural and historical context and the complex nuances that clarify them. Instead, they frequently quote scripture out of context, misrepresenting God as a hateful and vengeful deity eager to punish humans for the slightest mistakes or indiscretions. However, this portrayal is far from the truth.

God is not mean or hateful; His character embodies love and compassion. He desires that none suffer or perish, as stated in Ezekiel 18:32: "I take no pleasure in the death of anyone… Repent and live!" This challenges the notion of a vengeful God. The true God of scripture is often misunderstood. Unlike humans, He does not repay evil or hold grudges. He is righteous and loving, even toward those deemed unlovable. Furthermore, 2 Peter 3:9 emphasizes that the Lord is patient and wishes everyone to repent rather than perish.

Due to the widespread ignorance about scripture, many people require explanations and clarifications of biblical texts. Such clarification is vital because few have been taught that certain aspects of scripture address specific groups while others are meant for everyone. Nonetheless, it is essential to recognize that the guiding principles of scripture are constant and applicable to all. Consequently, reading scripture, attending Bible study, conducting scholarly research, and utilizing biblical commentaries are essential for achieving a deeper and more comprehensive understanding. Additionally, joining a theologically sound, Bible-believing church with solid teaching is crucial for enhancing spiritual depth and knowledge of scripture.

Personal Bible study is vital for spiritual growth and development. Simply engaging with scripture on Sundays without dedicating personal time to truth-seeking is inadequate. Failing to regularly interact with God's Word leaves us susceptible to misleading and false teachings. When we establish a habit of spending time in God's Word and presence, we learn to recognize His voice and understand His nature and character.

The word of God transcends being just a religious text; it serves as a crucial lifeline and source of strength for believers. God's word empowers, guides, and uplifts us, revealing the path to a life rich in strength, peace, power, and love. His words are reliable and never fail. Through His word and Spirit, God communicates with all who place their hope in Him.

God's word guides believers, teaching us to live righteously and serve others. It is a light in a dark world, restoring our hope, encouraging us in difficult times, and offering comfort during our brokenness. Engaging with Scripture revitalizes our souls and reaffirms that our present circumstances are fleeting; our true home lies in God's Kingdom. This engagement deepens our desire to connect with our Savior, beautifully reflected in Psalm 73:26: *"Though my mind and body may grow weak, God remains my strength; He is all I need."* This verse reminds us that in our moments of vulnerability, we can rely on His unwavering guidance, strength, and presence.

As followers of Christ Jesus, we are called to live differently, seek God in every aspect of our lives, and avoid selfish ambitions. Philippians 3:18-20 warns that some live as enemies of the cross, focusing solely on earthly desires. In contrast, those who live by faith, as described in

Hebrews 11:16, look toward a better, heavenly homeland. This perspective encourages us to live purposefully, grounded in eternal hope. The Word of God is a powerful tool for transformation. Studying God's Word produces a measurable change in our character and identity. Through transformation, things that once seemed important—prestige, status, position, and societal worth—become less significant. This shift occurs as we grasp the immeasurable and eternal value of what awaits us in Christ Jesus.

God's word inspires us to bring souls to His Kingdom. This divine purpose guides the lives and missions of all believers. Nothing is more significant, meaningful, or essential than leading souls to the kingdom of God and rescuing the lost from darkness. As the writer of Proverbs 11:30 wisely states, "*Those who win souls are wise, and the seeds of good deeds become a tree of life.*"

## Prayer:

Father, thank you for your word, which is a vital guide for my journey as a follower of Christ. Help me remember my purpose to share your grace, compassion, and mercy. Strengthen me during trials and temptations, and may I hide your word in my heart to share the truth with others in need. In the Mighty Name of Jesus, I pray, Amen!

## Meditating Scriptures:

**Matthew 24:35** – "Heaven and earth will disappear, but my words will never disappear."

**Psalm 119:105** – **"Your** word is a lamp to my feet and a light to my path."

### Key Points and Reminders

- Study God's word daily to deepen your relationship with Him
- Become more than just a reader of God's word; strive to be a student and doer
- Invest in quality scholarly resources, including commentaries, study Bibles, and faith-based materials
- Be diligent and intentional in learning and understanding scriptural text history, background, audience, cultural context, and purpose

# Reflection

No hurt, pain, or problem is too great for Christ to heal. If we want fulfillment, joy, and peace, we need the Lord Jesus even more.

# DAY 3
# INTENTIONALITY

**James 4:8:** "Come close to God, and God will come close to you."

---

I remember admiring those who had a genuine love for the Lord. Their bold and unapologetic faith inspired me as they pursued God and faced life's challenges with grace. Instead of fear or worry, they praised Him even in dark times, glorifying God regardless of their circumstances. Their goal was clear: to please God and honor Him despite any situation, and their lives reflected the declaration of Philippians 3:8-9: *"Everything else is worthless compared to the infinite value of knowing Christ Jesus my Lord. For his sake, I have discarded everything else, counting it all as garbage, so I could gain Christ and become one with him."*

What initially drew me to my husband was his authentic relationship with God. His unwavering faith and trust were remarkable, revealing an intimacy with the Lord I had never witnessed. I've come to understand that such a connection demands intentional effort. David beautifully described this in Psalm 63:1-8:

"O God, you are my God; I earnestly search for you. My soul thirsts for you; my whole body longs for you in this parched and weary land without water. I have seen you in your sanctuary and gazed upon your power and glory. Your unfailing love is better than life itself; how I praise you! I will praise you as long as I live, lifting my hands to you in prayer."

I recognize that those who genuinely know and love God often develop intentional habits. They meditate on His Word, pray regularly, immerse themselves in Scripture, and dedicate time to Him, even amidst their busy lives. Building a strong connection with God demands effort and a genuine sense of purpose, like any meaningful relationship. We can experience His incredible love, joy, and peace by nurturing our relationship with Him.

Life is filled with challenges, uncertainties, and fears. This world can be intimidating and seem hopeless, especially for those who do not know or believe in Christ. For those without Christ, life can be perpetually scary and frightening. However, living in constant fear is more than just an emotion; it is the work of a dark and demonic spirit that seeks to rob us of our peace and joy. Fear stands in opposition to peace and happiness. Fear and doubt represent the plan and actions of Satan, opposing the will of God. As 2 Timothy 1:7 reminds us, "God has not given us a spirit of fear and timidity but of power, love, and self-discipline." We do not have to remain in fear, worry, or anxiety. We can overcome fear by praying and turning to God's word for truth.

If we stay close to the Lord Christ, nothing can defeat us. Our most important relationship is with Him, who stands by us in every situation and circumstance. He will never abandon us and is truly our friend. Through this relationship, I have discovered that I don't have to wait for Heaven to experience power and intimacy with God; I can have it now. Because of this, I have witnessed and experienced countless blessings and marvelous things He has done.

Reflecting on my past, I realize that God instilled a desire to know Him intimately many years ago. I once admired others from a distance, and now I joyfully acknowledge that God has made me an example for many. By His grace, I've become even more than what I once admired. Glory be to the Lord Jesus Christ. Though I'm still growing, God continues to shape and mold me into the vessel He intends me to be, like clay on the potter's wheel. I will continue to be intentional about spending time in His presence, ready for His plan.

## Prayer:

As a brother or sister in Christ, I pray that the Word dwells in your heart, transforming and healing you. May you fulfill God's purpose and grow in spiritual closeness. Lastly, I pray you offer God the best part of your day. May this prayer guide your journey. In Jesus' Mighty Name, Amen.

## Meditating Scriptures:

**Psalm 145:18** – "The Lord is close to all who call on him, yes to all who call on him in truth."

**Matthew 6:33** – "Seek the Kingdom of God above all else, and live righteously, and he will give you everything you need."

### Key Points and Reminders

- Be intentional in nurturing your relationship with Christ
- Cultivate intimacy and trust in the Savior
- Stay connected to Jesus, our source of strength

# Reflection

The Christian life can be lonely, challenging, and at times isolating. Following the Lord Jesus is not meant to be easy. Jesus reminded us that following Him requires daily sacrifice, surrender, and intentional service to live for God, no matter the cost.

# DAY 4
# TRUE WEALTH

**1 Timothy 6:7** – "Yet true godliness with contentment is itself great wealth. For we brought nothing into the world and cannot take anything out of the world."

The letter addressed to the last church in the book of Revelation (Laodicea) illustrates the condition of many Christians in the current end times. Unfortunately, many prioritize having attractive partners, having children, buying homes, pursuing materialism, and accumulating wealth. They mistakenly perceive the accumulation of material riches, status, and possessions as a sign of God's blessing and favor. Incorrectly, they equate worldly wealth, prosperity, and success with God's will and purpose for their lives. Regrettably, they seek to acquire temporal material possessions more than eternal fellowship with their Creator, Christ Jesus.

Christians should appreciate the immeasurable value of their position in Christ and recognize the sacrifices made by those who came before them for the Gospel. They must also understand and acknowledge the importance of spreading Christ's message to save souls. Unfortunately, in a world that drifts further from God, many compromise their spiritual commitment by conforming to worldly standards in pursuit of acceptance, prestige, and admiration associated with wealth. This pursuit contradicts Matthew 6:24, which states that one cannot serve God and wealth.

Acquiring wealth isn't entirely wrong. Material wealth is a blessing from God, as He desires to prosper those He loves. Money itself isn't evil, but the love of it can lead to wickedness. It's important to remember that money is just a tool, not something to be worshipped. The true purpose of wealth is to serve God's will and help those less fortunate, fulfilling specific needs along the way. However, we must not forget that God is the infinite source of all our needs, as mentioned in Proverbs 11:27: *"Those who trust in their riches will fall, but the righteous will flourish like foliage."*

Wealth is not inherently sinful, but it becomes a problem when it consumes our thoughts and diverts us from our spiritual connection. While working long hours or taking extra shifts may be necessary, our focus should not solely be on material possessions. We stray from our path when prioritizing wealth over nurturing our spiritual well-being and fulfilling our purpose. Anything that distances us from our relationship with God is misaligned with His will. As Matthew 6:19-21 reminds us, we should store our treasures in heaven, as true fulfillment comes from our connection with Christ. Jesus emphasized that we cannot serve both God and money, and in John 10:7-10, He offers the gateway to an abundant life that material gain cannot provide.

If the pursuit of money has replaced your passions and ambitions for Christ, you are headed for destruction. The Devil is behind this shift, distracting our attention and focus from God. While social media advises getting richer, few focus on deepening their relationship with Christ. This neglect is dangerous, as the kingdom of Satan promotes self-gratification and materialism in a world that often rejects the simplicity and humility of Christ. This is the system of this fallen and depraved world. In contrast, the Kingdom of God highlights humility, generosity, compassion for the lost, and love for fellow believers. Jesus emphatically said, "My Kingdom is not of this world!" In Mark 8:36-38, the author poses an important question: "What does it benefit a person to gain the whole world but lose their soul? Is anything worth more than your soul?" Pursuing and gathering worldly riches while neglecting a relationship with the living God, Christ Jesus, is unwise. Life is far too short. However, eternity is forever.

In this world, everything is temporary, and nothing lasts forever. True wealth lies in accepting Christ as our Lord and Savior and living a devoted life in His followership. The real richness comes from recognizing and embracing what Christ has accomplished for us on the Cross of Calvary. With His blood, He paid the ultimate price for our sins, a debt we could never repay. True wealth lies in the certainty of our eternal home, fashioned not by human hands but by God. We are called to fulfill the evangelist's mission, earning a reward more precious than gold. Remember that the riches of this world will fade away, but the treasures of the Kingdom of God endure forever.

# Prayer:

I pray that God, the creator of the universe, becomes your highest priority. May you recognize that life on Earth pales compared to His abundant life for His children in Heaven. Commit to serving Him and understand that the things of this world are temporary. Should everything be stripped away, may you find peace knowing He is more than enough. Worship God alone, not the creations of His hands. In Jesus' name. Amen.

# Meditating Scriptures:

**Matthew 6:21** – "Store your treasures in heaven, where moths and rust cannot destroy, and thieves do not break in and steal. Wherever your treasure is, there the desires of your heart will be."

## Key Points and Reminders

- Keep your treasures and wealth in heaven
- Be proud of being called and chosen by God
- Remember, nothing lasts forever, and heaven is our eternal home

## Reflection

Nurturing strong, positive relationships with family, friends, and acquaintances offers numerous benefits. Nevertheless, a relationship with the Savior, Christ Jesus, holds greater significance than any other.

# DAY 5
# THE NARROW GATE

**Matthew 7:13** – "You can enter God's Kingdom only through the narrow gate. The highway to hell is broad, and its gate is wide for the many who choose that way. But the gateway to life is very narrow, the road is difficult, and few ever find it."

To enter the kingdom of God, we must pass through the Narrow Gate. The requirements for entry are specific. Hope and faith in Christ Jesus are the only and essential keys. Only those who have accepted Christ received Him as Lord and Savior and acknowledged Him as the only hope and atonement for sin can enter. The Kingdom of God is reserved for a specific group—the redeemed of Christ alone. There is no salvation in any other way.

Once again, I assert that only those who believe in Jesus Christ as their Lord and Savior can enter the kingdom of God. Those born again experience a transformation of heart and mind—they have been renewed. As a result, they are committed to serving and living in a way that pleases a Holy and Righteous God, leading righteous lives and bearing spiritual fruit of every kind. Their commitment and dedication distinguish them for God's purposes. They are unapologetically Christian, never compromising their walk with Christ or living contrary to God's word, as many do.

The path of darkness is broad and easy to find. Unfortunately, many refuse to accept Christ as the only way to righteousness and Heaven, believing instead that they can find alternative paths. However, this is a foolish mistake. Jesus says in John 14:6, "I am the way, the truth, and the life. No one can come to the Father except through me." Many people falsely believe that simply being a "good person," donating to charities, adhering to religious practices, following regulations and laws, and maintaining high moral standards are sufficient to guarantee their eternal salvation. This idea is contrary to scriptural teaching, the word of God.

In this fallen world, many confidently draw from a diverse tapestry of religious traditions, incorporating practices like crystals, tarot cards, and astrology into their lives. Some embrace polytheism or recognize various deities, believing that no single religious perspective is inherently superior to another. However, despite these varied practices, Jesus Christ remains the one true path to the Father. Through Christ alone, we can attain reconciliation and stand blameless in the presence of God.

The path to truth is narrow, and entry into the Kingdom of Heaven is through the only door: Christ Jesus. There are no substitutes available. In Acts 4:10-12, the apostle Peter spoke to a crowd, declaring, "Let me be clear to all of you and the people of Israel: This man was healed by the powerful name of Jesus Christ the Nazarene, the same man you crucified, but whom God raised from the dead." The scriptures mention Jesus saying, "The stone that the builders rejected has become the cornerstone." Salvation is found in no one else. God has provided no other name by which we can be saved. We are saved only through the incomparable name of Jesus!

In our Western culture and society, absolutes seem to be non-existent. For many, everything is permissible. If something does not hurt, harm, or only mildly offend, then all lifestyles and choices are deemed acceptable: homosexuality, pornography, and various sexual perversions. Greed, fornication, adultery, and all forms of idol worship persist, all under the guise of the "free spirit" and personal truth. Westerners often embrace being "free spirits." However, this concept of the free spirit frequently acts as a license for many to live as they wish, often without considering eternal consequences.

Anton Lavey, founder of the Church of Satan, proudly stated about the organization, "To us, Satan symbolizes the essence of those who are carnal by nature—people who experience no conflict between our thoughts and feelings, who do not accept the idea of a soul imprisoned in a body. He (Lucifer) embodies pride, liberty, and individualism—qualities often labeled as Evil by those who worship external deities, who perceive a struggle between their minds and emotions." In contrast, Christians are criticized for thinking, acting, and living as believers and followers of Christ, defending their faith, and highlighting behaviors and lifestyles that directly oppose God's word. Consequently, many professing believers find it challenging to remain steadfast, uncompromised, and unapologetic in their beliefs and committed to glorifying God and Him alone. The surrounding world's pull, allure, and pressure lead many to succumb and live lives of lukewarm faith at best.

Following Christ can be challenging, especially when family and friends do not share our beliefs. Navigating conflicts that arise from ideas contradicting the Christian faith can be difficult. Striving to live a godly life and maintain a standard of righteousness may lead some to label us as judgmental, but we should expect this reaction in a fallen and sinful world. We should never be surprised or frustrated by it. Many people appear to be godly yet live in denial of God's transformative power. As Christians, we are called to be bold. Declaring the unwavering and unyielding truth of the Gospel and the message of Christ can cause many to stumble and become defensive about their lives and choices that go against the teachings of Scripture.

As followers of Christ, we must never waver. Despite facing name-calling, insults, and rejection, we must remain faithful as ambassadors of God. We must persevere regardless of the costs, trials, struggles, or difficulties we encounter. In Matthew 5:14-16, we are encouraged by the words, *"You are the light of the world—like a city on a hilltop that cannot be hidden. No one lights a lamp and then puts it under a basket. Instead, a lamp is placed on a stand, illuminating everyone in the house. In the same way, let your good deeds shine out for all to see so that everyone will praise your heavenly Father."*

## Prayer:

Father, thank you for your Word, which guides us to enter your Kingdom through the narrow gate of Christ Jesus. Please help us to live as steadfast believers, reading your Word for wisdom and direction. I pray for those reading this and that you lead them to the narrow gate, Christ, and open their hearts to receive light and life for their souls. In Jesus' Mighty Name, Amen!

## Meditating Scriptures:

**Hebrews 11:6** – "And it is impossible to please God without faith. Anyone who wants to come to him must believe that God exists and that he rewards those who sincerely seek him."

### Key Points and Reminders

- Always maintain hope and faith in the Lord Jesus
- Remain committed to Christ through your lifestyle
- Obey the Lord, for only those who follow Him belong to Him

# Reflection

Nothing can be hidden from God. No matter the circumstance or situation, He is always present. Since He is inescapable, we should present ourselves fully to EL-ROI (the God of Seeing).

## DAY 6
# KEEP GOD INVOLVED IN EVERYTHING!

**Psalm 31:14-15** – "But I trust you, O Lord, saying, "You are my God! My future is in your hands."

Walking with the Lord is a profound journey that often feels like a fairy tale. In moments of joy and peace, we confidently proclaim that everything He does is for our good. We worship Him, recognizing His greatness as He blesses our efforts and fulfills our dreams. He answers our prayers more often than we expect and gives us more than we deserve, showering us with His abundant blessings. During these times, thoughts of misfortune and sorrow are overshadowed by His favor and the depth of His presence. When we ensure that God is involved in every aspect of our lives, we can remain confident and continue to move forward with purpose, fully convinced of our future and the extraordinary path He has laid out for us.

When things are good, they are perfect. However, it's easy to serve and live for God when everything is pleasant and wonderful—when life is enjoyable. But how do we respond when we feel sad, hurt, lonely, or deeply disappointed? What do we do when God doesn't seem near but feels far away? What do we do when our prayers go unanswered, hardships persist, and nothing changes? Do we still trust Him? Do we still believe He is in control, even when we don't understand? As followers of Christ and children of the great King, we must keep Him at the center of our lives no matter how it appears. He never fails.

Acknowledging and understanding that things don't always go as planned is essential. However, our obedience and confidence in God must remain steadfast. We cannot abandon or turn away from God during struggles, challenges, and trials. Instead, we must challenge and confront our spiritual immaturity, reflect on the past, and acknowledge God's faithfulness, giving us the strength and courage to hold on to what we know to be true: God has not, will not, and cannot fail. No matter the situation or circumstance, He will come through.

Too often, we forget that God is perfect in all His ways and always knows what is best for us. The reality of His omniscience is undeniable, yet we allow doubt to creep in, questioning whether He might make mistakes in our lives. I understand these thoughts can arise, but we must rise above them. We cannot let our weaknesses and human frailties blind us to the truth: God is always there, in control, guiding, protecting, and leading us. Let's learn to trust His promises and anticipate the future He has in store for us.

I have often made plans expecting God to honor and support my good ideas. From my perspective, I believed God should bless me; after all, I included Him in my plans. More than that, why wouldn't He bless me? This was a good plan. Over time, I have learned that God's plans often differ from mine. During moments of frustration, God has lovingly reminded me of the countless times I have exclaimed, "Not my will but Yours." When I feel frustrated, angry, and self-focused, God presses in my spirit the words of Ephesians 2:10: "We are His workmanship, created in Christ Jesus for good works, which God prepared beforehand that we should walk in them." How quickly we forget that He is the Potter, and we are the clay. We have no right to question how He shapes, uses, or prepares us. He alone knows the future.

Every experience culminates with our personal growth and God's glory. Sometimes, we receive exactly what we desire; other times, we encounter unexpected challenges. It's important to remember that God is not a genie granting wishes; He is a guiding presence who helps us navigate our journey. Occasionally, God leads us down unexpected paths filled with twists, turns, and detours, ensuring we reach our goals and intended destination. Sometimes, He sets us on an incomprehensible journey, ultimately guiding us to something far greater than we ever imagined. We can always place our hope in God. The writer tells us in Proverbs 3:5-6: *"Trust in the Lord with all your heart; do not rely on your understanding. Seek His will in all you do, and He will show you which path to take."*

## **The Story**

I remember yearning for a specific job opportunity. I prayed earnestly, confident that God would honor my request. I visualized myself in that role, which brought me immense joy. After the interview and receiving positive, encouraging feedback, I felt the position was mine. I was ready to leave a job that didn't fulfill me. However, I didn't get the job, and it devastated me. That was a dark and challenging time. I cried and cried, but eventually surrendered and asked God to fulfill me with His perfect plan and future will for my life.

Five months later, God revealed His plan. Due to a parent's illness, a friend and colleague had to leave a position she had recently taken. She encouraged me to apply for the job, but I felt uncomfortable because it would require me to step out of my comfort zone, try something new, and challenge myself in areas where I felt unprepared. I prayed and asked God to open the door of opportunity if it was His will for me. I applied for the position and was hired shortly after. Although I got the job, I was terrified and had to trust God to help me navigate this new and uncharted territory. Nevertheless, He proved Himself faithful every step of the way. From start to finish, He consistently supported me, delivering and rescuing me in times of difficulty and need. No matter the circumstances, He has never failed.

The writer in Isaiah 55:8-10 states that the Lord's thoughts and ways are beyond human understanding. His thoughts are higher than ours, just as the heavens are higher than the earth. Looking back five years, I can't believe I felt unprepared for that new position. But praise the Lord. He knew better. In His sovereignty, He denied one opportunity to provide another that would sustain me through the COVID-19 pandemic and allow me to complete my graduate studies. He created an environment and space where I could achieve significant professional and personal goals. Repeatedly, He has shown He is gracious, kind, and worthy of all adoration and praise.

The plans and wisdom of God are beyond our understanding. During my time in this new position, I worked remotely for an entire year while my husband transitioned to a new church and pastoral role in a different location. I developed a strong reputation for my work ethic at my company and received three wage increases, a testament to God's amazing grace and favor. The great American pastor and missionary, A.W. Tozer, once said, "As we exalt God to the right place in our lives, a thousand problems are solved all at once." When we surrender to God's plan and will, we can trust that He will never disappoint us, knowing what we need before we ask. Conversely, when we place our hope and trust in Him, He consistently meets our needs and exceeds our expectations.

In His divine wisdom, God foresaw a time when I would need more flexibility in my work schedule, job expectations, and available resources. He understood the ideal job, role, and position that would keep me employed, even during the pandemic crisis. God always knows what is best for us, often before we realize it ourselves. This is what makes Him such a wonderful God and Father. Affirming His love, in Isaiah 65:24, the LORD our God says, "I will answer them before they even call me. While they are still talking about their needs, I will answer their prayers!"

We must never forget that everything falls into place when we put God first. Regardless of the situation, we should stay open to what God is doing in our lives, even when we don't fully understand it. His thoughts and plans are higher than ours, and we can confidently believe He will always exceed our expectations. God must be welcomed in every aspect of our lives.

The writer encourages us in Matthew 6:31-33: "Do not worry, saying, 'What shall we eat?' or 'What shall we drink?' or 'What shall we wear?' For the pagans run after all these things, and your heavenly Father knows that you need them. But seek His kingdom and righteousness first, and all these things will be given to you."

## Prayer:

Father, I pray that you continue to guide us in every step. I ask that your infinite wisdom and loving kindness remind and encourage us. Lord, I pray that we always obey, even when we do not understand what you are doing. Thank you for never failing us. Thank you for everything you do because everything you do is perfect. In Jesus' name, Amen!

## Meditating Scriptures:

**Psalm 32:11** – "So rejoice in the Lord and be glad, all you who obey him! Shout for joy, all of you whose hearts are pure!"

### Key Points and Reminders

- Even in testing, challenges, and trials, trust in God
- Never forget, He is the Potter, and we are the clay
- Trust that God knows best how to guide us toward our destiny and purpose

# Reflection

Too often, we feel abandoned or alone. However, that is never the case. We have a faithful friend in our Savior. Even in our darkest and most challenging hours, we have the unwavering assurance of Jehovah-Shamma, which means "The Lord is There," always present and supporting us.

# DAY 7
# PRAYER

**James 4:8** – "Come close to God, and he will come close to you."

Nothing in the universe compares to the extraordinary power of prayer. We can experience a remarkable and intimate connection with the Lord in prayer. In this form of worship, we dialogue with the Creator of all things. God has blessed us with this gift, allowing us to connect with the Sovereign at any time and place. Undoubtedly, prayer remains one of our greatest gifts. No other form of communication can measure up to it. Through His divine will, God has provided a way for us to draw closer to His infinite wisdom. Regardless of the time, place, situation, or circumstances, we can always reach out to Him. He neither sleeps nor slumbers and is always ready to respond when we call because He hears us.

Prayer lets us express our worries, frustrations, anxieties, and fears. It empowers us to overcome our adversaries' schemes. Through prayer, we can quiet competing voices and connect with the voice of life and truth. We draw from the ultimate source of wisdom, knowledge, and power necessary to change and transform our circumstances. Most importantly, prayer brings us closer to the might and power of the universe, teaching us to hope and trust in Him, the one who is faithful and true.

Sometimes, our expectations may not be fulfilled, which can result in feelings of disappointment. In such moments, we might lose focus and interest in prayer. However, we should never cease praying, as this is precisely what the enemy wishes. He aims to break our connection and fellowship with God, the source of life. No matter what happens, we must never stop praying.

In Philippians 4:6, the writer encourages us: "Don't worry about anything; pray about everything. Tell God what you need and thank Him for all He has done." God reminds us to persevere because He is faithful and merciful. He speaks to us, reminding us of His goodness through our time in prayer, the words of a friend or family member, a praise and worship song, or through His Word. The Scriptures encourage us to stay vigilant and persistent in prayer. In 1 Thessalonians 5:16-18, the writer advises us to "rejoice always, pray continually, and give thanks in all circumstances; for this is God's will for you in Christ Jesus."

As believers, we are fortunate to have the opportunity to approach God's throne in prayer with confidence, knowing that our requests and petitions are heard. We can trust that our loving and compassionate Father listens and responds to our needs. We should recognize that a delayed response does not equate to denial; God answers our prayers at the appropriate time. God is always on time—He is never late.

Although God may take longer than we would like, He is always at work. Often, He uses times of waiting to transform our attitudes and perspectives. He aligns our desires with His will, shifting our focus from problems to praise. God dwells in the praises of His people. Delays provide us with opportunities to gain new insights and experiences in Him.

It's important to understand that God tests our faith, patience, and obedience, often through delays. God frequently uses waiting to assess our motivation and willingness to keep seeking Him, even when things don't go as planned. Frequently, through delays, He tests our obedience and commitment to remain faithful, thankful, and appreciative while we await His response. God uses waiting as an opportunity to teach us the truth: He is not obligated to grant every request or conform to our ever-changing desires. On the contrary, He is the Creator, and we are merely His creation. No matter how long He takes, He will answer and, as always, exceed our expectations.

Prayer is essential for building a closer relationship with our God and Father. It is never futile; no plea goes unheard. God rewards those who remain faithful in prayer. Prayer is an act of faith and the practice of discipline. Through prayer, we demonstrate our hope and trust in God.

Because we believe in His power, we find comfort in Matthew 21:22: "Whatever you ask in prayer, you will receive, if you have faith." He will reward those who maintain their faith in Him and continually seek Him in prayer, even when His response seems delayed.

## Prayer:

Father, I pray those reading this will learn to pray in every circumstance. I pray that the gift of prayer becomes a life source for them and that they make prayer the foundation of their lives. God, let every word and petition be sincere, respectful, and filled with adoration toward You. Father, thank You for being so mindful of us. Thank You for giving us the gift of prayer to bring our concerns, fears, and requests to You. Lord, you are lovely, and we thank You. In Jesus' mighty name, Amen!

## Meditating Scriptures:

**James 5:13** – "Is anyone among you in trouble? Let them pray. Is anyone happy? Let them sing songs of praise."

### Key Points and Reminders

- Never cease to pray
- Keep persevering, even when God is silent
- Never lose hope. God is always faithful

## Reflection

As followers of Christ, we are called to fight. We cannot afford to be timid, hesitant, or cowardly in tough times. Even when we feel defeated, scared, or weak, we can rely on Jehovah-Eyaluth (My Help), our steadfast source of strength.

# DAY 8
# CLOSETED CHRISTIANS

**Acts 4:29 –** "And now, O Lord, hear their threats, and give us, your servants, great boldness in preaching your word."

Many followers of Christ keep their faith private and hidden, choosing not to display their commitments and convictions openly. Sadly, due to the fear of reaction and the potential ridicule of those around them, they are hesitant to share the power of the Gospel message in their lives and the lives of others. As a result of this fear, many spend their lives as "Closeted Christians."

Although salvation does not depend on public displays, we must recognize that God has not relieved us of our obligation to share the Gospel. Those called by the Lord into His service, saved by His precious blood and unimaginable grace, should deeply understand the Gospel's power. We are testimonies demonstrating how God can profoundly transform empty and broken lives. As believers and followers of the Lord Jesus, we are irrefutable witnesses to the Gospel message's power to transform and change lives. Because of this reality, all believers should be motivated and inspired to share their faith boldly and confidently.

As ambassadors of Christ, we should never hide our faith. We have been chosen to be His children, living epistles for God, and cannot be closeted Christians. On the contrary, God expects us to be bold and open about our hope in Him. We are called to be lights in the darkness, chosen people, God's elect, and cities on a hill that shines brightly. God requires us to live out our faith loudly, bravely, and boldly. In a world that parades and flaunts its rejection and disobedience, we must equally parade the irrefutable truth of the power of our God.

If we choose to follow Christ, we cannot remain hidden. We cannot conceal our faith. We must remember that one day, we will all stand before Christ, the great and righteous judge, and be accountable for our actions. Indeed, we will eventually give an account of everything we have done in this life, especially our testimony to our Lord and Savior. The writer strongly reminds us of the Savior's words in Matthew 10:32-33: "Everyone who acknowledges me publicly here on earth, I will also acknowledge before my Father in heaven. But everyone who denies me here on earth, I will also deny before my Father in heaven."

Regardless of where we find ourselves, we must never forget that time is fleeting, death is inevitable, and people need Christ more than ever. Chosen by God, we are responsible for sharing His message, especially with non-believers and those who have never heard the Gospel. Since time is short and eternity is inevitable, we cannot remain silent about our faith and hope in Christ Jesus, regardless of the cost. In 2 Timothy 2:11-12, the author states, "This is a trustworthy saying: If we die with him, we will also live with him. If we endure hardship, we will reign with him. If we deny him, he will deny us."

While we may fear conflict, rejection, and insult, we should fear the denial of our Creator even more. The writer encourages us in Luke 12:4-5, "Dear friends, don't be afraid of those who want to kill your body; they cannot do any more to you after that. But I'll tell you whom to fear. Fear God, who has the power to kill you and then throw you into hell. Yes, he's the one to fear." We cannot afford to be lukewarm. Our faith must be all-encompassing. We must be fully committed to Christ.

In a world that grows darker and more depraved each day, filled with moral confusion and despair, we are called to share the transformative message of Christ with boldness. This involves living out our faith authentically and speaking boldly and passionately about the hope that comes from a relationship with Christ Jesus. We cannot hide our beliefs; they are meant to shine brightly and light the way for others who need purpose and salvation.

Following Christ comes at a cost. We must be ready to face the consequences of our choices. Regarding this, Jesus said in Luke 14:26-27,

"If you want to be my disciple, you must, by comparison, hate everyone else—your father and mother, wife and children, brothers and sisters—yes, even your own life. Otherwise, you cannot be my disciple. And if you do not carry your cross and follow me, you cannot be my disciple."

Rejection is part of the Christian experience. Living boldly for God comes at a price. However, no matter our sacrifices, we still fall short of Christ's sacrifice at Calvary. Because of Christ's matchless sacrifice, we owe Him everything. He paid a debt He did not owe. Sinless, He died for the sins of many. The writer records the words of the Savior in John 15:13-14: "There is no greater love than to lay down one's life for one's friends. You are my friends if you do what I command."

The world is filled with countless broken and confused individuals. Many willingly embrace falsehoods and distortions, striving to create self-serving realities. Given this, we should view it as an opportunity to share the freedom found in Christ Jesus. The eternal destinies of many men and women depend on our courage to boldly convey the message of salvation, regardless of the cost or consequences. In 1 Peter 3:15-16, we are encouraged to honor Christ and to be prepared to explain our hope with gentleness and respect. As followers of Christ Jesus, we are directed to spread the message of hope to all nations. We cannot conceal our faith; we must emulate our Savior, even at significant personal cost. We will not withhold the truth if we love those around us—family, friends, and close acquaintances. We cannot sit passively by and allow them to be lost. The great evangelist Billy Graham once said, "Our faith becomes stronger as we express it; a growing faith is a sharing faith." As children of God, we do not have the luxury of living as "Closeted Christians." Jesus said in Matthew 28:19-20, "Go and make disciples of all the nations.... Teach these new disciples to obey all the commands I have given you." We are called to action, and we must obey!

## Prayer:

Father, please grant us strength, courage, and boldness to speak the truth in a dark, evil, and depraved world. Help us never to be ashamed of the Gospel, as we know it brings eternal life to those who believe. Father, I pray that the Holy Spirit gives us wisdom to discern how and when to speak. Please help us continue showing grace and mercy to those newly on their journey and walking with You. Remind us, O Lord, of Your grace. Heavenly Father, we humbly seek Your strength, courage, and boldness to proclaim Your truth in a world shrouded in darkness. In Jesus' Name, I pray. Amen.

## Meditating Scriptures:

**Psalm 111:8** – "The Lord is for me so that I will have no fear. What can mere people do to me?"

### Key Points and Reminders

- Never be ashamed of your hope in Christ
- Live your faith boldly
- Fully commit to Christ

# Reflection

God is in control of our lives. He is the author of the days, weeks, and years that have passed and those that lie ahead. We can have unwavering confidence, hope, and faith in Him. He is EL Shaddai, God Almighty, God All-Sufficient, and everything He does is excellent.

# DAY 9
# A DAILY WALK

**Jeremiah 29:13** – "You will seek me and find me when you seek me with all your heart."

---

Witnessing someone fully surrender their life to the Lord and experiencing God's transformative work is a beautiful and unforgettable experience. It is incredible to observe the dramatic, life-changing shifts in their choices from embracing a new life filled with obedience, dedication, and reverence for God. This transformation often arises from recognizing the emptiness that exists without Him. As fellow believers, we should feel immense encouragement and joy when we witness God's transformative power in another person's life. Each experience is a powerful reminder of God's amazing grace, showing that He does not show favoritism based on position, rank, or status; there is always room at the cross for one more.

The life of a believer is filled with purpose. Our purpose is to preach, teach, and reach out to win souls for the kingdom of God. From a Christian perspective, there is no greater joy or satisfaction than witnessing the lost emerge from darkness into the light of the Lord Jesus Christ. The goal of soul-winning is the aspiration of all believers. A believer's purpose is found and defined in Jesus' command: "Go and make disciples of all nations, baptizing them in the name of the Father, the Son, and the Holy Spirit, and teaching them to obey everything I have commanded you." This is not a suggestion; instead, it is the commandment of our LORD.

As followers of Christ, we are called to share His transformative message. Jesus is the definitive path to heaven. In His conversation with the religious leader Nicodemus, He stated in John 3:3-7, "No one can see the Kingdom of God unless they are born again," meaning being born of water and the

Spirit. Through the Holy Spirit, we experience spiritual rebirth. To worship God, we must do so in spirit and truth. The Lord our God is Spirit.

The Christian life unfolds moment by moment and day by day, with each day offering distinct choices and decisions. As His followers, we must intentionally and proactively make space to hear His guiding whispers. He speaks softly to our spirits, continually leading us in the right direction. Although distractions may try to pull us off course, it is vital to stay focused, as this not only helps us excel in our work but also deepens our connection with Him.

Every day, we should make time to connect with the Lord. Starting our day in His presence prepares us for the challenges ahead. Let God's Word guide you, as the psalmist says in Psalm 119:103-105, "How sweet your words taste to me; they are sweeter than honey. Your words are a lamp for my feet and a light for my path."

## Prayer:

Father, I pray that your will and purpose for your followers here on Earth are fulfilled. May your will be done on Earth as it is in Heaven. I pray that we all submit to the call and use every gift you have given us to win souls for your Kingdom. In Jesus' name, amen!

## Meditating Scriptures:

**Psalm 14:2** – "The Lord looks down from heaven on all mankind to see if there are any who understand, any who seek God."

### Key Points and Reminders

- Everyday living for Christ is a new experience and adventure
- Be a soul winner; that is our true purpose
- Begin each day in communion with Christ

# Reflection

The deceiver's schemes are many. The only way to avoid them is to draw near and remain close to God. Trust in the Great IAM is well-founded and never in vain.

# DAY 10
# VALIDATION

**Colossians 3:23** – "Whatever you do, work heartily, as for the Lord and not for men, knowing that from the Lord you will receive the inheritance as your reward."

Have you ever thought about why we seek validation from others? In my experience, the need for approval from family, friends, and colleagues has dramatically influenced my life. This quest has posed many challenges, teaching me valuable lessons about my motivations. Ultimately, I've understood that others' approval is unimportant; what truly matters is the Lord's approval and belief in what and who He says I am.

I've learned that seeking recognition from others can lead to disappointment. While wanting acknowledgment is natural, it often results in pain. Not everyone will celebrate your achievements, which has taught me the value of self-acceptance and intrinsic motivation. I've cultivated self-awareness and resilience through setbacks, enabling me to celebrate my successes.

Dealing with family rejection is challenging and often frustrating. Not everyone can genuinely celebrate your successes, especially when you achieve more than they do. This has caused me much pain and sadness, but I've learned to seek validation from the Lord, as His acceptance is what truly matters. I've grown to move past the need for familial recognition, yet it can still be problematic when others receive the praise they don't deserve while my efforts still go unnoticed or acknowledged.

The desire for appreciation is fundamental to human nature, but relying on external validation can lead to disappointment. Grounding ourselves in God's Word affirms our identity in Christ, helping us develop a more profound sense of value and worth. The apostle Paul encourages us to prioritize God's approval over the approval of others, which leads to greater fulfillment in our spiritual journey. In Galatians 1:10, he states, "I am not trying to win people's approval, but God's approval."

As followers of Christ, we should seek validation that aligns with God's Word rather than the fleeting opinions of others. While it is natural to desire validation, reflecting on our motivations is essential. Without the guidance of the Holy Spirit, unchecked motives can easily lead us into the traps of ego and pride, preventing God—who is the only one genuinely worthy—from receiving all the glory and honor. We can embrace His good and perfect will by allowing God's Spirit to lead and guide us.

Many people pursue their desires and ambitions without realizing or discovering God's plan, resulting in dissatisfaction and unfulfillment. They often miss the transformative power of the Holy Spirit and overlook God's active role in their lives. Living outside of God's will forfeits the blessings He has for us. God offers more than the world's fleeting pleasures, as stated in 1 John 2:16, which warns that the world's offerings are not from the Father. As believers, we are called to obey God's commands, as noted in 1 John 2:15, which cautions against loving the world. Ultimately, neglecting to walk in God's light leads to darkness.

Friends, we must understand that seeking acceptance from the world can endanger our spiritual journey with Christ. If we're not careful, we risk our eternal souls for the fleeting applause of a decaying world. People's opinions are trivial compared to eternity. As Matthew 10 tells us, we should not fear those who can harm our bodies but revere God, who holds power over our souls. Ultimately, God's opinion truly matters; only His judgment carries the weight of eternity.

In Mark 8:36-37, we are reminded of the importance of our souls: "What good is it to gain the whole world, yet forfeit your soul?" Our identity and validation should be rooted in Christ. 1 John 2:24-25 emphasizes the need to remain faithful and maintain fellowship with the Son and the Father. As God is our hope for salvation, seeking His approval should be our primary focus. Ultimately, our goal must be to hear our God say, "Well done!" as we fulfill His purpose.

## Prayer:

Father, as your devoted followers, we confidently seek to please you and value your approval above all else. Remind us that our primary mission is to share the gospel of Jesus Christ with boldness and passion. Holy Spirit, empower us to live as dedicated Christians, walking humbly before you in all we do. We will not seek the approval of others, for our focus is solely on you. In Jesus' Name, Amen!

## Meditating Scriptures:

**Galatians 1:10** – "For am I now seeking the approval of man, or God? Or am I trying to please man? If I were still trying to please man, I would not be a servant of Christ."

### Key Points and Reminders

- Pursue validation and approval from God alone
- Uphold God's standards and reject worldly practices and behaviors
- Do not attempt to serve both God and material possessions

# Reflection

It is unwise to believe or assume that everyone is guaranteed Heaven. This idea contradicts scripture. Without holiness, no one will see God. Only those washed by the blood of the Lamb are made righteous and accepted by EL Elyon, God Most High.

# DAY 11
# SOMETIMES FAMILIES DON'T UNDERSTAND

**2 Peter 1:10** – "Therefore, brothers, be all the more diligent to confirm your calling and election, for if you practice these qualities, you will never fall."

In my life, I have faced significant disappointments, mainly related to my family, which sometimes led me to wish I belonged to a different one. Despite the heartaches and betrayals, I've continued to trust God, believing He is all-knowing. While I've felt frustrated and thought I could have made better choices, I've understood that His ways and thoughts are higher than mine. If this is the family He gave me, it was to bring Him glory and to accomplish His perfect will.

From the outside, my childhood appeared perfect. My parents worked hard, and we lived comfortably with my two siblings. However, beneath this façade, we faced a cycle of dysfunction that profoundly affected our lives.

I don't mean to be harsh or judgmental. My parents did their best despite their challenging upbringings with abusive parents. They worked hard to provide opportunities for my siblings and me. Given their struggles, they did an exceptional job. Unfortunately, their experiences resulted in lives that lacked real substance or a genuine foundation in Christ.

Like many children, I grew up in a Christian household where faith often felt hollow, impacting my emotional well-being as I observed my family's struggles. Our focus on materialism and competition strained our unity and support. Despite these challenges, I love my family and believe that God brought us together, even if I sometimes question His reasoning. I trust in His sovereignty.

Meeting my husband, a devoted man of God, has truly transformed my life. Relocating has allowed me to recognize my family's dysfunction and embrace a much-needed, peaceful lifestyle. In the past, without a solid foundation or relationship with Christ, I was focused on my desires, which caused me to lose sight of my purpose and drift further away from God. However, this journey has deepened my faith and enriched my relationship with the Lord, and I am incredibly grateful for this change!

Navigating life with my spouse and family has deepened my appreciation for grace and forgiveness. Trusting in God's plan has taught me to view challenges as growth opportunities, relying on His strength. These experiences have transformed our relationships, uplifted my spirit, fostered healing, and helped us move beyond past hurts.

Since surrendering my life to Christ, I've faced ridicule and judgment from my family, who seem to resent my transformation. They dismiss my progress and even claim my husband has brainwashed me. Despite their mockery, my faith remains strong. I love my family, but my love for Christ comes first.

God has transformed my life in incredible ways. After ten years of following Christ, my love for Him remains strong. Those who once doubted my faith are now more accepting, and some seek my guidance as they start their journeys. I am grateful to be used by Him, no matter how small the way. All glory and honor go to Him.

Many of my loved ones have not accepted Christ, choosing worldly pleasures over the hope He offers. In the words of Jackie Hill-Perry, "You will turn from your sin when you discover that Jesus is better than anything you have ever loved." God can reach those who resist through the Holy Spirit and transform chaotic lives. Out of love, I continue to pray for their salvation, hoping that God will save them one day.

# Prayer:

Father, I pray for my family and the person reading this who has had a similar experience along their spiritual journey. Please grant them the needed strength and encourage them as they continue their journey. Lord, make their transformation easy, evident, and convincing so naysayers yield to your will. Let our lives demonstrate and exemplify goodliness and uncompromised living. In Jesus' name, Amen!

# Meditating Scriptures:

**John 17:3** – "And this is eternal life, that they know you, the only true God, and Jesus Christ whom you have sent."

## Key Points and Reminders

- Do not hold on to the past (Let go)
- Forgive and move forward
- There is always hope in God

# Reflection

We are called to be lights amid immense darkness. The Way stands in stark contrast to the emerging world around us. Following Christ means being different, standing out, and facing disdain due to our commitment to the Lord. We should never find it strange when rejected for our hope and faith in Christ. If we are hated because of Christ, we must remember that the world hates and continues to hate our Savior.

# DAY 12
# MAKE JESUS A DAILY CHOICE!

**Colossians 2:6-7** says, "So then, just as you have received Christ Jesus as Lord, continue to live in him, being rooted and built up in him and established in the faith, just as you were taught, and overflowing with gratitude."

Today and every day, remain steadfast in your identity in Christ. Remember, prioritizing the kingdom over worldly, carnal, and temporary things is crucial and helps keep us centered on our true purpose. The Bible reminds us in Philippians 4:8 to focus on authentic, noble, pure, lovely, admirable, excellent, and praiseworthy things. Lucifer, the Devil, tries to divert us by attacking our minds. He uses a time-tested strategy of recalling our past mistakes, condemning us, and whispering lies. If we are not vigilant, this can lead to sadness, bitterness, and despair. We must consciously guard our minds and concentrate on heavenly things that further the Lord's kingdom.

Recognizing that our thoughts inspire our actions, we must dedicate time to God daily, finding a distraction-free environment. This practice deepens our faith. By consciously allowing ourselves to be guided by the Holy Spirit, we gain valuable wisdom and direction, reassuring us that we are never alone on our spiritual journey. The Holy Spirit is a steadfast companion, guiding us along the path of righteousness.

As children of the Great King, embracing forgiveness can profoundly transform our lives and deepen our relationship with God. We are encouraged to forgive others, follow the guidance of Christ Jesus, pray for those who may have wronged us, and genuinely seek to clear up any grievances when forgiveness is offered. True forgiveness means letting go of hurt and receiving others as if the offense never occurred. Just as God has extended grace to us, we are called to share that same compassion. Embracing forgiveness demonstrates our strength in Christ, enabling us to manage our emotions and respond gracefully. Ultimately, this practice can transform relationships and promote healing in our lives and communities.

In times of difficulty, we may feel unworthy and seek guidance. By placing our faith in Christ Jesus, we can gain confidence in His unwavering love. Following Christ opens the door to eternal life and strengthens our faith journey. Although we may feel powerless, through Him, we can find the strength to navigate challenges, stand firm in our beliefs, and avoid paths that conflict with His teachings and demands for our lives.

Choosing Christ is a daily decision, even in hopeless times. As believers, we walk by faith, trusting in the impossible because we are children of an all-powerful God. With faith and courage, we can embrace the truth that, in Christ Jesus, all things are possible. The Bible assures us that we are victorious through Christ, who has already won the battle on the cross.

As children of God, we hold a remarkable position. According to 1 John 5:4-5, faith empowers us to overcome the world's darkness. While we achieve victory through Christ, it requires intentional choices and effort. We must nurture our faith daily, trust His power, and apply God's word. By prioritizing Jesus above all else, we can and will triumph over the challenges and wickedness of this world.

## Prayer:

Lord Jesus, I pray you would help us choose you daily. Father, please guide us to see, understand, and accept the plan, will, and purpose you have ordained for us since our creation despite the many temptations, enticements, and distractions that come our way. Choosing you is the best, most fulfilling, and most rewarding way to live. Please guide our steps and lead us daily by the spirit of truth, Lord Jesus. I pray for all of this in your Mighty Name, Amen.

## Meditating Scriptures:

**Hebrews 12:1-2** – "Therefore, since we also have such a large crowd of witnesses to the life of faith, let us strip off every weight that slows us down, especially the sin that so easily trips us up. And let's run with endurance the race God has set before us."

**John 14:26** – "**But** the Advocate, the Holy Spirit whom the Father will send in my name, will teach you all things and remind you of everything I have said to you."

### Key Points and Reminders

- Prioritize time with God through Bible study, prayer, and quiet reflection
- Practice forgiveness for yourself and others
- Practice healthy spiritual disciplines and routines daily

# Reflection

When we feel lost and lack trust in others, the words of Christ Jesus, our Lord and Savior, can provide us with hope, comfort, and guidance.

# DAY 13
# DON'T BE DECEIVED

**Proverbs 14:12:** "There is a path before each person that seems right, but its end is the way of death."

It's all too easy to fall into the deceptive trap of the world, seduced by the fleeting comforts and conveniences that life offers us. In doing so, we risk denying our inherent need for and dependence on God. We often find ourselves drawn away from a deep and meaningful relationship with God by the allure of wealth, social standing, and recognition from others. We may mistakenly believe these measurable and tangible blessings are definitive indicators of God's approval and favor.

The belief that material possessions reflect God's blessings can be misleading. It often distracts us from core spiritual values and commitments. In pursuing personal gain, we may overlook essential obligations, like nurturing our relationship with God and sharing His message with others.

When materialism takes priority, we overlook our true purpose: serving the Lord Jesus Christ. We forget that we are temporary pilgrims in a foreign land, losing sight of our limited time here and our faithful citizenship in a kingdom that transcends our current circumstances.

As we journey through life, we should remember our primary goal: returning home to God. This perspective helps us focus on what truly matters and strengthens our faith amidst distractions. Too often, we prioritize material possessions over spiritual growth. With limited time, it's essential to realign our priorities to actions that hold lasting significance.

For ages, the enemy has used material gain to lead those seeking a godly life away from the light. Satan even attempted this tactic against the Savior. In Matthew 4:8-11, the devil showed Jesus all the world's kingdoms, promising them in exchange for worship. Jesus rebuked him, saying, "Get away from me, Satan! It is written: 'Worship the Lord your God and serve Him only." The devil then left, and angels came to attend to Jesus."

Satan boldly seeks to deceive us, underscoring the importance of remaining vigilant in our faith. Understanding our adversary helps us resist his temptations. While he offers false treasures like Fool's Gold, God provides true riches to those who trust Him. Staying rooted in our faith allows us to recognize and cherish God's gifts. As James 1:17 reminds us, "Every good and perfect gift is from above." The Spirit of God works in our lives, promoting goodness and spiritual transformation.

The culture emphasizes individualism and self-absorption, steering our focus from God's transformative word to social media. This shift leads us to seek validation through likes and shares, fostering a cycle of narcissism that distracts us from our spiritual lives. As we spend more time online, we drift from our Savior and neglect essential practices like prayer, Bible study, reflection, meditation, and personal spiritual growth.

Disconnection from God makes us vulnerable to Satan's deceptions and unhealthy desires. While the devil seeks to diminish our joy, God remains in control. We can enjoy life, including social media and movies, but we must ensure they don't overshadow our relationship with the Lord. Balance is essential.

Jesus Christ exemplifies how to resist temptation and face evil and weakness. We must refocus on what matters, reclaim our spiritual lives, and stand firm against distractions from our loving Savior and God.

# Prayer:

Father, I pray for your protection from the traps, snares, and lies the enemy uses to deceive us into thinking we do not need you. Lord, we desperately need you. Help us not to be drawn away from you by all the enticements of this life. Father, if anything comes between our relationship with you, I ask that you be gracious and kind to remove whatever stands in the way of our commitment to serving you alone. In Jesus's name, Amen!

# Meditating Scriptures:

**1 Timothy 4:1:** "Now the Holy Spirit tells us clearly that in the last times, some will turn away from the true faith; they will follow deceptive spirits and teachings from demons. These people are hypocrites and liars, and their consciousnesses are dead."

### Key Points and Reminders

- Reject and resist selfish desires and passions
- Satan, our adversary, never rests and is the greatest of deceivers
- Oppose the schemes of Satan using the Word of God

# Reflection

Value and worth should never be determined by human perspective or opinion. Only Yahweh (God) can give us worth, purpose, and value.

# DAY 14
# THE PURSUIT OF HOLINESS

**Proverbs 11:23:** "The Godly can look forward to a reward, while the wicked can only expect judgment."

Have you ever considered what it means to be holy? A great example is Christ Jesus, who embodies true holiness. The Bible calls us "holy" in all we do, as stated in 1 Peter 1:16: "You shall be holy, for I am holy." While holiness may seem like a lofty goal requiring perfection, it ultimately centers on our relationship with God and His Christ.

As believers, we are called living sacrifices, actively pursuing God's holiness. This journey should inspire us, as it allows God's love and grace to foster our growth and deepen our connection with Him. Holiness is not just an option; it is the divine standard inviting us to be set apart for His purpose.

As His cherished possession, we are called to daily crucify our flesh and surrender to the Lord's will. We can demonstrate this by putting others before ourselves and allowing our love to shine through our actions. Embodying kindness, grace, and compassion in every situation while committing to fast from distractions to prioritize our time with God is essential. Surrounding ourselves with fellow believers can inspire us to stay accountable and uplift our actions and behavior.

The Lord Christ is our sinless Savior, and God, our heavenly Father, is supreme and eternal. Through His boundless love, Christ has freed us from the penalty of sin. Hebrews 10:14- 19 states that Jesus' single offering has perfected those being sanctified. The Holy Spirit confirms that God will instill His laws in our hearts and forget our sins. No further sacrifices are needed; we can boldly enter Heaven's Most Holy Place through Jesus' blood.

As God's emissaries, we confidently embrace a transformative intimacy and fellowship that shape us into His likeness. As His children, we are called to reflect His character through our actions and conduct without reservation. We honor Him by boldly living out His righteousness and holiness, steadfastly rejecting the corrupt ways of this fallen world.

We should regularly reflect on key questions in our pursuit of holiness and our desire to please God. How do I interact with (non-believing) neighbors? Is there a noticeable difference between the way we conduct our lives? Do I feel superior to those who are less successful? Is my help to others genuinely selfless? How do I react to mistreatment? Am I focused on my own needs or those of others? Am I honest in my self-evaluation? Am I ready to meet the Lord? As followers of Jesus Christ, we must confront these questions with intention and determination.

As we follow Christ, we must ask ourselves: Am I living a life that pleases God? Am I intentionally sharing the Gospel with non-believers? If asked, can I explain my hope in Christ Jesus? Am I seeking daily to be filled with the Holy Spirit for the work He has called me to do? Without God's power, fulfilling Christian standards is impossible. As David expressed in Psalms 42:1-2, "As the deer longs for streams of water, so I long for you, O God."

Living for God requires submitting to Him and striving for a life of complete holiness. 1 John 3:9 highlights that those born into God's family do not engage in sin because God's life dwells within them. Our assurance of our identity as children of God comes from the Holy Spirit's conviction of hidden sins, which motivates us to repent and turn away from wrongdoing. Those born of God respond to the Holy Spirit by surrendering, repenting, and distancing themselves from anything that displeases Him.

In contrast to unbelievers, whose hearts are darkened by sin, our nature is different. Romans 6:5-8 tells us, "Since we have been united with Him in His death, we will also be raised to life as He was. Our old sinful selves were crucified with Christ, so we are no longer slaves to sin."

God has empowered us to discern right from wrong, freeing us from being controlled by our flesh and desires.

A key challenge in our spiritual journey is recognizing our imperfections. Acknowledging our shortcomings reveals our need for the Holy Spirit's guidance. Yielding to His leadership involves being open to His prompts, trusting Him, aligning with His presence, resisting temptation, and making choices that reflect our commitment to God's will.

Surrendering our lives to Christ allows His Spirit to guide us, freeing us from sin's control. The Holy Spirit convicts us when we err, returning us to God. This is the journey of redemption and growth.

# Prayer:

Father, I pray that holiness becomes the intentional standard for every believer and follower of Jesus Christ. Please help us live uncompromised in our walk and commitment to You. Father, I pray that a dedication to living holy, righteously, and fully submitted to Your perfect will consume all Your children. In Jesus' mighty name. Amen!

# Meditating Scriptures:

**Proverbs 12:28:** "The way of the godly leads to life; that path does not lead to death."

## Key Points and Reminders

- Strive for God's holiness
- Emulate the example of Christ Jesus
- Stay humble and let Christ be the source of strength

# Reflection

God is gracious and kind to us daily, and we should be genuinely grateful. Not only for the immeasurable physical and spiritual blessings He has so lovingly granted us but also because, by His unmerited favor, He provides us with countless opportunities to make Him the center and focus of our lives.

# DAY 15
# THE FAVOR OF THE LORD

**Psalm 90:17:** "Let the favor of the Lord our God be upon us and establish the work of our hands upon us; yes, establish the work of our hands!"

Many Christians respond, "I am blessed and highly favored." What does that mean? This notion of being "favored" suggests being held in high regard and reflects God's presence and power in our lives. Favor implies more than material blessings; it encompasses divine protection, peace, security, and joy. Ultimately, favor represents God's unearned and undeserved grace at work.

In Psalms 37:23, the writer states, "The steps of a man are established by the LORD when he delights in his ways." This verse teaches us that when our lives align with God's will, and we actively apply His word, He provides us with clear direction and guidance, reflecting His favor upon us. While God always desires to bless and prosper us, this does not mean we will be free from hardships.

Scripture presents individuals like Noah, Moses, Joseph, Job, Daniel, Jeremiah, and Paul, who faced significant challenges despite receiving God's favor. Their stories show that God's favor doesn't shield us from hardships but sustains and guides us through trials. This reinforces the belief that God's favor provides protection, purpose, and direction, inspiring trust in His plan even amid adversity.

The favor of God is a gift granted when we genuinely surrender to Him, loving Him with all our being (Mark 12:30). In response to His grace, we should live righteously and work to advance His kingdom. Although we are undeserving, maintaining pure intentions and a spirit of gratitude is essential, as God sees our hearts. Psalm 5:12 reminds us, "Surely, LORD, you bless the righteous; you surround them with your favor as with a shield."

Putting our relationship with the Lord above our desires pleases God and invites His favor. By making God the center of our lives and nurturing that connection, we cultivate wisdom during struggles and find joy in challenging times. A life grounded in Christ Jesus leads to the rewards of His good and perfect gifts.

## Prayer:

Father, we approach you with grateful hearts as we celebrate your abundant favor! Lord, I pray that every reader of this book will develop a deep relationship with you and fully experience your grace. May they earnestly seek your presence in all aspects of their lives, aligning their motives with your divine will. Guide them toward righteous living and inspire a heart that longs for you. In Jesus' Name, Amen.

## Meditating Scriptures

**Isaiah 66:2:** "These are the ones I look on with favor, those who are humble and contrite in spirit, and who tremble at my words."

### Key Points and Reminders

- Live by God's will
- God's power and the demonstration of His favor are limitless
- Prioritize pleasing God

## Reflection

The LORD, Jehovah-Kadosh, the Holy One, is a wise Master. He has given us the treasure of His Holy Spirit and the strength needed for every good work. We have no excuses because He has given us the power to fulfill His perfect will. He expects a return on His investment. We must win souls. Failing to honor the trust placed in us is unacceptable, whether intentional or unintentional.

# DAY 16
# PREACH, TEACH, OR REACH!

**Mark 16:15** – "And he told them, "Go into all the world and preach the Good News to everyone. Anyone who believes and is baptized will be saved."

My husband, Reverend Dr. Scott, recently delivered a powerful sermon titled "What Are You Going to Do? Preach, Teach, or Reach, but you must do something." This poignant message made me reflect on the importance of acting as preachers, educators, advocates, or simply as friends and family. Each of us has a unique role in influencing those around us, whether through social media, guiding our children, or supporting our loved ones. We all have a role and responsibility within our unique spheres of influence.

As followers of the Lord Jesus Christ, we must influence others thoughtfully and responsibly. Our words and actions reflect our faith and can positively affect those around us. We can cultivate kindness, spread hope, and foster change aligned with our values. Our primary objective is to be the Lord's representative and bring someone closer to Him.

As we go through our daily lives, we should consider the influence we choose to have and the steps we can take to make a difference. Proverbs 12:26 says, "The righteous are a guide to their neighbor, but the way of the wicked leads them astray." How does this resonate with you?

Reflect on your life and your impact on the community. Consider whether your actions align with scripture and promote involvement in God's kingdom. This is an opportunity for personal and spiritual growth, especially during challenges. God calls us to use our unique talents and resources wisely, making this journey of self-reflection, analysis, recognition, and maximizing our gifts an ongoing experience and exercise.

We are accountable for how we use our abilities and opportunities. It's essential to reflect on whether we fully utilize our gifts and uplift others. Consider how you can contribute to God's kingdom and positively impact those around you. This reflection can renew your purpose and deepen your faith.

One day, all will see God. Christians will stand before the Bema (the Mercy seat), receiving rewards for advancing God's kingdom, while those unsure of their salvation will face the Great White Throne of Judgment (Revelation 20:11-12). Consider these questions: Have you served the Lord fruitfully? Are you investing in discipleship? Do you have the assurance of salvation through Christ, or have you turned away?

# Prayer:

Father, I pray for the reader of this book. May You meet their needs and open their hearts, allowing them to experience Your presence. Transform each heart, for You are the only hope of salvation and eternal life. God, I ask that those who feel discouraged continue to preach, teach, and reach others, leading them to You. In Jesus' mighty name, I pray. Amen!

# Meditating Scripture

**James 5:19-20** – "My dear brother and sisters, if someone among you wanders away from the truth and is brought back, you can be sure that whoever brings the sinner back will save that person from death and bring about the forgiveness of many sins."

## Key Points and Reminders

- Share the Gospel message with people everywhere
- Help others understand that there is no hope of salvation without Christ
- Help others become ready and prepared to stand before God

# Reflection

Excuses are among the many tools of the lazy and uncommitted. No reason will be sufficient when we stand before Him. We have either obeyed, or we haven't. Laziness is, and will always be, the fuel of disobedience and a barrier to closely and intimately knowing Yeshua, our Savior and Messiah.

# DAY 17
# SPIRITUAL LAZINESS

**Proverbs 16:17:** "The path of the virtuous leads away from evil; whoever follows that path is safe."

Many individuals who identify as Christians today expect God to fulfill their requests instantly, treating Him more like a personal genie than as their Lord and Savior. This has resulted in a neglect of essential spiritual practices such as Bible study, reflection, meditation, and prayer, leading to apathy and spiritual laziness among many believers.

Far too many church believers lack a genuine connection with God, showing a concerning commitment to prayer and Scripture. Christians must go beyond superficial labels and actively invest in their faith to deepen their relationship with Christ, embracing the transformative power of true communion with Him.

In today's culture, many self-identified Christians lead undisciplined, prayerless lives, struggling with a lack of power and peace. True peace comes only through Christ, the Prince of Peace. Spiritual laziness prevents them from fully committing and growing in God's truths.

Spiritual laziness results in a refusal to seek essential resources, like Bible study and faith-based literature, which deepen understanding of God's truths. Many neglect the opportunity to connect with more mature believers who could aid their growth. It's crucial to recognize these priorities now, hold each other accountable, and awaken those who are spiritually slumbering.

Spiritual discipline and commitment are essential for experiencing the blessings of a Christian life. A relationship with Christ instills confidence in our prayers as He responds to those who approach Him with hope and faith. However, those who are spiritually lazy shouldn't expect to receive anything from the Lord. Proverbs 15:29 reminds us, "The Lord is far from the wicked, but He hears the prayers of the righteous." God is loving but owes nothing to those who neglect their relationship with Him.

The Christian life often clashes with worldly values. In 1 Timothy 4:7, we are urged to "Train yourselves to be godly," highlighting the need for disciplined effort to honor God. Godliness provides lasting rewards and empowers us to reflect on His light and love in a needy world. We must fully commit to honoring our Father and avoid spiritual complacency.

The Christian life is a transformative journey that requires discipline and purpose. We strive to be like our Savior and confront falsehoods amid a culture focused on fleeting desires. As we strive to live righteously, we aim to reflect God's glory through spiritual discipline. In 1 Timothy 4:14-16, Paul encourages Timothy to honor his spiritual gift and focus on his responsibilities, emphasizing the importance of living and teaching rightly for his salvation and the salvation of others.

As children of the Great King, we are responsible for winning souls for God's kingdom through preaching, teaching, and outreach. As Christ's emissaries, we must take up our cross daily, follow Him, and resist selfish desires. To truly belong to Him, we must acknowledge and intentionally walk in His Spirit. Engaging in spiritual disciplines is essential for knowing and pleasing God, and we must avoid spiritual complacency to experience all He has for us.

## Prayer:

Spirit of the Living God, I ask for your blessings upon those who genuinely desire to live lives dedicated to you. I pray that your Holy Spirit, our constant companion, will continue to lead and guide them as they surrender their lives and wills to you. Father, please help those who are spiritually complacent and lack the desire to read and study your Word. Grant them the motivation and discipline to seek you daily. In Jesus' name, Amen.

## Meditating Scriptures

**2 Timothy 2:15-16:** "Do your best to present yourself to God as one approved, a worker who does not need to be ashamed and correctly handles the word of truth. Avoid godless chatter because those who indulge in it will become increasingly ungodly."

**1 John 1:9:** "If we confess our sins, he is faithful and just to forgive us our sins and cleanse us from all unrighteousness."

## Key Points and Reminders

- Avoid spiritual complacency
- Engage in spiritual disciplines
- Don't overlook the study of God's Word

# Reflection

Death is an unavoidable reality for everyone. Each day brings us closer to our destined encounter. Those who have placed their hope, trust, and faith in Christ Jesus eagerly anticipate that blessed moment. When the ties that connect us to this world are severed, we will find ourselves in the presence of our God, Jehovah-Tsaddiq, the Righteous One.

# DAY 18
# THE UNEASY PATH

**2 Corinthians 12:9** – "My grace is all you need. My power works best in weakness."

---

Becoming a Christian can be challenging and requires discipline, a commitment to God's word, and a willingness to make sacrifices. It often involves facing opposition, ridicule, and feelings of loneliness. I have faced many of these struggles myself, and while they can be painful, they have also strengthened my faith and convictions. You are not alone on this journey—these challenges can lead to meaningful growth and resilience. Once we accept Christ as our Lord and Savior, He promises to be with us always, never leaving or abandoning us.

Under most circumstances, no one wants to suffer or endure abuse, hardships, or persecution. However, this should be the expectation of Christians. Following the Lord Jesus is an unavoidable reality. The writer notes in 2 Timothy 2:12, "Everyone who wants to live a godly life in Christ Jesus will suffer persecution." Suffering in various forms for our faith is part of the journey in The Way. There are no exceptions. We are reminded in 1 Peter 4:1-4, "Since Christ has suffered in His body, we must be ready to suffer also." Suffering brings an end to sin.

Believers in Christ are often unfairly viewed as judgmental or divisive, leading to sadness. While other faiths receive recognition, Bible-believing Christians striving for righteousness frequently face ridicule and rejection. This painful reality has echoed throughout history and continues to affect many today.

When facing struggles, it's essential to approach them with an open heart. Maintaining faith in a hostile world can be difficult. In John

15:18-21, Jesus reminds us that the world's animosity toward us stems from its animosity toward Him. We are not of this world, and the Holy Spirit is essential for enduring challenges and fulfilling God's calling as His witnesses.

Following Christ comes at a cost. It is not for the faint of heart or the timid. In Luke 14:26-27, Jesus said, "If you want to be my disciple, you must, by comparison, hate everyone else—your father and mother, your wife and children, your brothers and sisters—yes, even your own life. Otherwise, you cannot be my disciple. And if you do not carry your cross and follow me, you cannot be my disciple." The Christian life demands sacrifice.

Before becoming a Christian, reflect on your beliefs and commitment to serve the Lord. This journey depends on the Holy Spirit's power. Jesus states in Luke 24:49, "I will send the Holy Spirit... stay here until He fills you with power." Acts 1:8 adds, "You will receive power when the Holy Spirit comes upon you." Fulfilling God's perfect plan and will is impossible without the Lord's power. We need His Spirit.

Choosing to follow Christ can feel isolating, but He offers peace and solace in our struggles. His strength is sufficient in our weakness; we're not meant to walk this journey alone. We find the strength to carry on through the love and power of His Holy Spirit.

## Prayer:

Father, thank you for being the perfect example of endurance and a source of comfort during times of suffering and distress. Lord, I praise you for extending grace and mercy toward us each day. Father, I pray for your continual strength. God sustains our faith to believe even when everything within us challenges that belief. Please help us to live fully for you. In Jesus' Name, Amen

## Meditating Scriptures:

**Romans 8:18** – "Yet what we suffer now is nothing compared to the glory he will reveal to us later."

### Key Points and Reminders

- Be ready to bear the cost of living the Christian life
- Embrace rejection and loneliness with joy
- God will support us in our weakness

## Reflection

The life devoted to Christ differs from the many lives chosen by the masses. The life of a follower of Jesus is neither a sprint nor a marathon; it is a life of daily, intentional, measured, and calculated decisions that involve self-denial, sacrifice, and surrender.

# DAY 19
# DRIFTING AWAY

**Psalm 25:4-5** – "Make me know your ways, O Lord; teach me your paths. Lead me in your truth and teach me, for you are the God of my salvation; for you, I wait all day long."

Have you ever noticed a decline in your desire to spend time with the Lord? I've experienced this, too, facing seasons of reduced enthusiasm for studying His Word and praying, often accompanied by shame and anxiety. However, these moments drove me to reassess my priorities and seek Him more intentionally. This lack of intimacy inspired me to reconnect, engage in fellowship, and practice spiritual disciplines, ultimately transforming sadness into joy.

When I disconnect from God, old feelings and pains often resurface. If you feel this way, you're not alone. It's tough when Satan uses our past mistakes against us, but God doesn't want that for us. Recognizing these attacks is the first step to overcoming them. Engaging with God's Word, praying, and seeking fellowship with other believers can help us stay strong. No matter what comes or what attack the enemy launches, we must remember that we have God's strength to resist and overcome.

We all have mountaintop moments that make us feel invincible, but staying close to God during these times is crucial. Complacency can weaken our prayer life and leave us vulnerable to the enemy. As 1 Peter 5:8-9 warns, we must remain alert, resist the devil, and stand firm in our faith, knowing fellow believers face similar challenges.

As Christians, we must acknowledge and recognize that true peace and joy come only from God; Jesus is the Prince of Peace. We must embrace that the world's fleeting pleasures leave us empty, while only through Him can our deepest needs be met. The writer affirmed this reality in Psalm 16:11, "You will show me the way of life, granting me the joy of your presence."

We often drift from our connection with God despite His desire for closeness. This occurs due to our human weaknesses and selfish choices. The Apostle Paul expressed similar struggles in Romans 7:19-20, highlighting the need for God's power to live righteously and please Him. As we distance ourselves from God, worldly influences become overwhelming. Drawing closer to God strengthens our ability to resist these influences. In contrast, spending time with Him helps us reflect on His character and access His powerful spirit, enabling us to live righteously and resist self-centeredness and pride.

God loves us and desires to spend time with us. As a compassionate Father, He welcomes us back, no matter how far we stray. Our identity is rooted in Him, and we should be grateful for His love. Romans 8:38-39 emphasizes God's unwavering love: "Nothing can ever separate us from God's love... not even the powers of hell."

Maintaining a connection to God is essential, but many people struggle with this due to the demands and distractions of daily life. We must prioritize our relationship with Him, as He is the ultimate source of life and strength. By acknowledging our weaknesses and seeking His presence, we can receive God's grace to live by His will and walk righteously before Him. It is not God who abandons us; we tend to drift away when we neglect our fellowship with Him.

David expressed the importance of this connection in Psalm 27:4, emphasizing his desire to dwell in the Lord's presence and seek Him daily. He stated, "The one thing I ask of the Lord—the thing I seek most—is to live in the house of the Lord all the days of my life, delighting in the Lord's perfections and meditating in His Temple."

# Prayer:

Father, in your unmatched name, I ask that you remain in us and that we remain in you. I pray that you keep us close and prevent us from drifting away. Please keep us in your presence. Thank you for loving us so profoundly and allowing us to experience you in our times of need. This reminds us that you are the source of everything we hope for, desire, need, and imagine. Father, let our hearts yearn for you more and more, in Jesus' name. Amen!

# Meditating Scriptures:

**Romans 8:1** – "There is no condemnation for those in Christ Jesus."

## Key Points and Reminders

- Stay close to God
- Stay vigilant. Be aware of the schemes and traps of the devil
- Devote as much time as you can to God

# Reflection

Jesus commanded us to be, do, and go. There is no room for excuses. We must follow His example, striving to fulfill and carry out God's will, purpose, and plan. To follow Christ, we must be ready to leave everything behind, fixing our eyes on the kingdom and the eternal reward of heaven.

# DAY 20
# CHILDREN DERAILED

**Psalm 65:1-3 –** "What mighty praise, O God, belongs to you in Zion. We will fulfill our vows to you because you answer our prayers. All of us must come to you. Though we are overwhelmed by our sins, you forgive them all. What a joy for those you bring near, those who live in your holy courts."

As we observe the present state of our world, it's clear that Christ's return is imminent. Many have heard this message, and current events suggest it could happen sooner than expected. We see a rapid decline in moral and spiritual values; many have strayed from righteousness. Now, more than ever, we must realign our priorities and refocus on Christ's return.

Many have turned away from the truth, viewing the God of the Bible as an afterthought. Spiritual blindness has led to interest in alchemy, astrology, tarot, and witchcraft practices. Consequently, being a Bible-believing Christian is often mocked. Isaiah 5:20-23 warns, "What sorrow for those who call evil good and good evil, who substitute darkness for light... who are wise in their own eyes and think themselves clever."

Many people around the world are straying from the core teachings of the Bible, embracing personal interpretations that often lead to a superficial identification as Christians. A closer look at their lives can reveal hypocrisy and inconsistency with Scripture. The writer argues that not everyone claiming to follow Christ is genuine, as Jesus warns in Matthew 7:21-23, "Not everyone who calls out to me, 'Lord! Lord!' will enter the Kingdom of Heaven... But I will reply, I never knew you. Depart from me, you who break God's laws."

The distance from God's righteousness is evident today, with frequent portrayals of same-sex relationships on television reflecting a rejection of His original design. The LGBTQA+ agenda is prominent across platforms, and children now grow up in a world that feels unfamiliar and hostile. They are increasingly exposed to sensual content, which seems to have damaging consequences.

Today, children have access to activities like consuming alcohol and smoking marijuana at home, often justified by parents who prefer their kids doing it safely rather than on the streets. While many project an image of piety, they overlook the transformative power of God. This compromise has led to fewer individuals truly embracing biblical truths, contributing to a society that increasingly tolerates harmful behaviors and risks heading toward destruction.

Many children today grow up in households where religion is optional, resulting in a lack of essential knowledge about God. This trend makes them vulnerable to misleading ideologies. We must actively teach our children about prayer, scripture, and the importance of community worship. If we believe in the power of God's Word, we cannot be passive; we should create environments that nurture faith and encourage open discussions about God.

The drift from God is unsurprising, as Scripture outlines expectations for Christ's return. In 2 Timothy 3:2-4, it's stated that people will become lovers of themselves and money, boastful, disobedient, ungrateful, and lacking self-control. They will be cruel, betray friends, and prioritize pleasure over God.

## **My Story**

Growing up, my family attended church without understanding the importance of a personal relationship with the Lord. The pastor focused on strict rules, labeling many behaviors as sinful without explanations, leading to confusion. It wasn't until later that I realized the value of nurturing a genuine relationship with God that encourages inquiry and embraces His love and grace.

I've realized that God despises sin, which deepens my appreciation for Christ's sacrifice. Although my parents didn't share this with me, I learned the importance of building a relationship with the Savior through the Word of God. As I grew in understanding, I discovered the incredible power of God's love and the power of the Holy Spirit to help us break free from sin.

Before God's revelation, I misunderstood spiritual commitment and the Holy Spirit's role in guiding repentance. I found salvation in Christ through God's grace, realizing I cannot earn His love or forgiveness. My righteousness is not based on good deeds; it relies entirely on God's grace through faith in Christ. This truth lets me approach God confidently and humbly, deepening my relationship with Him as my source of strength.

In Ephesians 2:2-10, the writer emphasizes God's immense love, stating that we were once dead in our sins and lived in disobedience, following our sinful nature. However, God, rich in mercy, loved us so much that even though we were dead in our sins, He gave us life by raising Christ from the dead. We are saved only by His grace.

Recognizing that I can approach God boldly in my mistakes has been transformative. I can walk in Christ without fear, knowing His love embraces us despite our failures. Asking for forgiveness reassures me of His willingness to provide it. Being open with God is powerful, as He understands our struggles and encourages us to bring our challenges without shame. In His presence, I find grace that empowers my journey toward a more profound, authentic faith. God meets us where we are, guiding us toward healing and renewal.

Struggles highlight the beauty of our journey. Rather than succumbing to high expectations, we can see challenges as chances to grow closer to God. Our weaknesses show our need for His support. This journey is not about perfection but about deepening our relationship with Him. By acknowledging our limitations and focusing on God, we find the strength to move forward. Each stumble invites us to embrace His grace and transformation.

God, in His love, never leaves us without support. He sends help through the individuals who teach us about His character and how to live the Christian life. When we are open and ready, He provides the guidance we need through fellow believers who help deepen our relationship with Him. Great is His faithfulness; He knows how to reach His children, no matter their journey. Praise the LORD, our God and Savior, Jesus Christ!

## Prayer:

Lord, you are faithful. Thank you for bringing us back when we stray and for the gift of reconnection through your Son, Jesus Christ. I pray for the readers, encouraging them to follow you with open hearts. May they repent and seek your guidance. Let their loved ones witness your transformative power and choose to follow you. In Jesus' name, Amen.

## Meditating Scriptures:

**Acts 17:30-31** – "In the past, God overlooked such ignorance, but now he commands everyone everywhere to repent. He set a day to judge the world with justice by the man he appointed. He has given proof of this to everyone by raising him from the dead."

**1 Chronicles 28:9** as if speaking to their child, "As for you, my son Solomon, know the God of your father, and serve Him with a whole heart and a willing mind; for the Lord searches all hearts, and understands every intent of the thoughts. If you seek Him, He will let you find Him; but if you forsake Him, He will reject you forever."

### Key Points and Reminders

- Stay focused on God and avoid distractions
- Cling to the standards of God and the truth of His Word
- Embrace your weaknesses, turn to Christ, and be righteous through Him

# Reflection

For most, life can feel like a vast sea or ocean in which we are all adrift in various directions of uncertainty. Indeed, we cannot know what tomorrow has in store. However, we who place our hope in God understand who holds our future, Adonai, and it will be well. He is the LORD and Master, and He cannot lie.

# DAY 21
# A TIME FOR REFLECTION

**2 Timothy 3:16**- "God inspires all Scripture, and it is useful to teach us what is true and to make us realize what is wrong in our lives. It corrects us when we are wrong and teaches us to do what is right."

The 'Parable of the Sower,' also known as the 'Parable of the Farmer's Scattered Seed,' serves as a key theme for reflection, vividly illustrating the transformative power of God's word. In this parable, Jesus uses the seed as a metaphor for the Word of God and describes its effects when it lands on different types of soil, which symbolizes the state of the heart. In His analogy, Christ identifies three kinds of soil representing people, highlighting the impact of God's Word on our lives.

The first type of soil is rocky ground, symbolizing those who receive God's Word with great joy. However, the message doesn't take hold as intended because they lack deep roots in Scripture. As a result, they quickly fall away when faced with trials and challenges. Satan snatches away the message and the power of the Word from their hearts, preventing them from genuinely believing and being saved. While these individuals may attend church and listen to inspiring sermons, their inability to pray and spend quality time with God regularly hinders the growth of their relationship with Him. This ultimately leads to a lack of faith and unnecessary struggles during difficult and distressing times.

The second type of soil described by the Savior is found among thorns. This thorny soil symbolizes individuals burdened by worries, the pursuit of wealth, and personal pleasures, all hindering their spiritual growth. Their faith is weakened, lacking the necessary development and maturity to bear good fruit. They mistakenly believe superficial service to God will grant them their wishes like a genie. These individuals seek only what they can gain from God instead of surrendering to His will and committing themselves to His service.

The soil referred to as "good ground" symbolizes individuals with honest hearts who receive the word of God, hold onto it through challenges, and bear godly fruit. These individuals maintain the right attitude and are open to learning and spiritual growth. They regularly seek God's presence, attend Bible studies, and engage with His word. With this positive mindset, they actively participate in church and worship services, expecting to hear a message from the Lord while prioritizing time spent with fellow believers. Moreover, they are mindful of their social media usage, concentrating on spiritual matters rather than distractions. They are intentionally kingdom-minded and committed to their spiritual development and growth. This is the will of God and the expectation of all believers and followers of our Lord Christ Jesus.

Mature Christians hold tightly to what they have learned, even in trials. True believers face challenges and difficulties with steadfast hope and trust in God, discovering joy regardless of their circumstances. Spiritual maturity is essential for aligning with God's perfect will, even when His plan is unclear. Scriptures teach that children of light can be recognized by the fruit that appears in their lives. Just as all trees are known for the fruit they produce—an apple tree does not bear figs, nor does an orange tree bear lemons—believers are identified by their actions and conduct. In Galatians 5:22-23, the writer states that the Holy Spirit cultivates love, joy, peace, patience, kindness, goodness, faithfulness, gentleness, and self-control in the life of a believer. So, I ask you, which qualities are manifested in your life?

# Prayer:

Lord, help us to be like the seed that falls on good soil. Help us produce good and godly fruit. As your children, guide and lead us. Help us become everything you created us to be and nothing less. Instill in us a desire for your perfect will over our own. Let us be a sweet sacrifice to you in Jesus' name. Amen.

# Meditating Scriptures:

**Luke 8:4-8** – "A farmer went out to plant his seed. As he scattered it across his field, some seed fell on a footpath, where it was stepped on, and the birds ate it. Other seeds fell among rocks. It began to grow, but the plant soon wilted and died of lack of moisture. Other seeds fell among thorns that grew up with it and choked out the tender plants. Still, other seeds fell on fertile soil. This seed grew and produced a crop a hundred times as much as had been planted!"

## Key Points and Reminders

- Do not let your faith be lost or shipwrecked
- Focus on what is profitable and beneficial for the kingdom of God
- Strive for spiritual maturity, letting the Word of God take root in the good soil of your heart

# Reflection

There are numerous paths and routes to take, but without Christ, they ultimately lead to nothing. There are countless paths to destruction. Jesus alone is the way, the truth, and the life.

# DAY 22
# THE UPS, DOWNS, AND FLOW OF LIFE

**1 Peter 2:21** – "To this, you were called, because Christ suffered for you, leaving you an example, that you should follow in his steps."

Life is full of ups and downs—good days and bad, sunny times and rainy seasons, peaks and valleys, ebbs and flows. Yet, one thing remains constant: God's unchanging nature. We can find comfort in this truth. God does not change. He is faithful even when we are not, reliable when we fail, and strong in our weakness.

It is essential not to take God's grace for granted. His grace is not a free pass to sin but a testament to His undeserved kindness. Because of His goodness and mercy, God deserves our obedience, regardless of our feelings or justifications for our actions. Even when we fall short of His expectations, He extends grace and kindness. Through His love and compassion, He spares us from the punishment we deserve and blesses us in ways we cannot earn or repay. God is consistent and immeasurable in His favor toward us. Reflecting on God's goodness and grace, the writer of Proverbs 18:10 states, "The name of the Lord is a strong tower; the righteous run to it and are safe."

When life feels overwhelming, it's important to remember that we have a choice. We can either allow ourselves to be consumed by emotions such as sadness, discontent, and frustration, or we can seek solace in distractions like drugs, alcohol, or entertainment. We also have the potential for another choice. We can turn to the hope that is in Christ Jesus. I have learned that true comfort, satisfaction, and peace come from placing all hope, faith, and trust in God. As the book of Psalms reminds us, "The LORD gives strength to his people; the LORD blesses his people with peace." This is a powerful reminder that we can choose God as our source of comfort and peace, regardless of our challenges.

In Luke 15:10, we learn that when a sinner repents, there is rejoicing and jubilant celebration in the presence of God's angels. John Newton's hymn "Amazing Grace" describes his salvation experience through God's grace. This grace taught him to fear the Lord and relieved him of worldly fears. Similarly, when I came to believe and hope in Christ, God's grace became precious. Newton's experience resonates with me because God's grace transformed my life when I surrendered and dedicated myself to Christ. I, too, became a new creation, leaving behind my former ways and actions of the past.

As a born-again believer in Christ Jesus, I am deeply devoted to the Word of God. It is the source of my strength and sustenance for my life. Every day, I make it a ritual and a habit to find a quiet space, pray, meditate on His Word, and listen to God's gentle voice. We do not see God in the rolling thunder, lightning, earthquake, or raging winds. Instead, it is often within the quiet and stillness. The prophet Elijah supports this insight with his own experience. The writer records in 1 Kings 19:11-13:

"As Elijah stood there, the Lord passed by, and a mighty windstorm hit the mountain. It was such a terrible blast that the rocks were torn loose, but the Lord was not in the wind. After the wind, there was an earthquake, but the Lord was not in the earthquake. And after the earthquake, there was a fire, but the Lord was not in the fire. After the fire, there was the sound of a gentle whisper. When Elijah heard it, he wrapped his face in his cloak and went out and stood at the entrance of the cave. And a voice said, "What are you doing here, Elijah?"

We must learn to wait patiently and actively listen for God's voice, even when it doesn't come in ways we expect, especially during distress. In moments of great need, I've found that seeking the Lord and being patient is our safest refuge. He is our strong tower where we can find peace, comfort, and rest. Life is riddled with challenges, but Christ Jesus assures us we need not worry. We have the privilege of approaching Him and finding solace in His presence. The writer's words in 1 Peter 5:7 encourage us: "Give all your worries and cares to God, for He cares about you."

Surrendering control to God and allowing Him to fulfill His perfect will in our lives can be one of the most liberating feelings and acts of freedom.

Experiencing God's grace has brought profound transformation to my life. Time and again, He has orchestrated and arranged situations that have compelled me to surrender and trust Him. Through these experiences, I have found Him to be a reliable refuge and anchor amid struggles. As one of His children, I find comfort in Psalm 46, which declares, *"God is our refuge and strength, an ever-present help in trouble. Therefore, we will not fear, though the earth gives way, the mountains fall into the heart of the sea, its waters roar and foam, and the mountains quake with their surge. The Lord Almighty is with us; the God of Jacob is our fortress."*

## Prayer:

Father, I come before you, honoring and revering you for being a saving grace in our lives. I pray that when our circumstances weigh us down, you will continue to be the rock on which we stand. Remind us of your word; let us taste and see that you are good in every trial. Inspire us to have faith without limitations or borders, empowering us to face any challenge with confidence in you. In Jesus' Name, Amen!

## Meditating Scriptures:

**1 Peter 4:19** – "So if you are suffering in a manner that pleases God, keep doing what is right, and trust your lives to the God who created you, for he will never fail you."

### Key Points and Reminders

- Trust in God and find peace
- Pay attention to the voice of God every day
- Trust that even during difficult times, God is present

# Reflection

The word of God is far more precious than diamonds, rubies, and even the most expensive pearls. The words of EL-Olam (The Everlasting God) serve as the source of life for our souls.

# DAY 23
# ESSENTIAL TO THE FAITH JOURNEY: RELATIONSHIP WITH GOD

**John 17:3** - "And this is eternal life, that they may know you, the only true God, and Jesus Christ whom you have sent."

We must surrender our lives to God's Lordship and align with His purpose and will. By renewing ourselves in Christ, we can gain a deeper understanding of His plans, allowing us to participate with clear focus, direction, and intention. By embracing God and drawing closer to Him, we create an opportunity for Him to work through us, guiding us to fulfill His good, pleasing, and perfect will, even in challenging circumstances.

The writer of Proverbs 3:5-6 encourages us to trust the Lord with all our hearts and not to rely solely on our understanding. We are urged to seek Him in all our ways, and He promises to guide us on straight paths. While many often quote verse 5, verse 6 is even more important as it reminds us that our goal should be to know God and to trust Him to direct our paths.

Many people find it difficult to invite God into their lives, having been in control of their existence for too long. It's essential to recognize the value of seeking His guidance, especially when making critical decisions about finances, careers, or choosing a life partner. Turning to God for direction in our decision-making can help us navigate challenges and manage uncertainties. It is wise to consult the Lord in every situation. By bringing our worries, interests, and concerns to Him in prayer, we create an opportunity for God to guide our choices and share His wisdom, helping us to achieve clarity and purpose.

In times of tragedy and loss, it is common to question the nature and character of God. We may wonder why an all-powerful God didn't prevent our suffering. While it can be challenging to accept this, it doesn't change the fact that He is both omnipotent and all-knowing. There is no situation or circumstance of which He is not aware. He is always in complete control. Those who have not come to know Christ and accept His sovereignty often struggle with doubt and worry, primarily because they neglect prayer, fellowship, and studying His Word. As a result, they miss out on the peace that comes from developing a deeper relationship with Him and the confidence and assurance of His promises and faithfulness, no matter the situation.

It is important to remember that God's ways differ from ours, and He is always at work and ideally in control of every scenario. As followers of Christ, we are not exempt from trials, heartaches, and pain. Yes, even Christians face struggles. However, we have hope. We trust in God's perfect wisdom, even when we cannot understand His plan. We do not grieve as the world does. Our faith, confidence, and hope remain firmly placed in our God.

As Christians, we recognize that death is an inevitable part of the human experience. Since God is the Creator and Author of life, He has the right and privilege to give and take life as He sees fit. Unlike those who do not share our faith, we, as believers, navigate challenges, struggles, and varying degrees of grief in unique ways. Despite our circumstances, we continue to serve, believe, and trust in God, even during the most difficult times. We affirm that He is good, even when we feel disappointed, frustrated, angry, and sad.

Experiencing loss can be incredibly heart-wrenching. However, regardless of the circumstances, we always hold on to hope. As believers, we find comfort in 1 Thessalonians 4:13-14, which reassures us that even if a loved one passes away, we will see them again when Jesus returns. The writer comforts us by saying:

*"Dear brothers and sisters, we want you to know what will happen to the believers who have died so you will not grieve like people who have no hope. For since we believe that Jesus died and was raised to life again, we*

*also believe that when Jesus returns, God will bring back with him the believers who have died."*

During complex and challenging times, we should not mourn as those without faith. As followers of Christ, we understand that death does not hold the final authority. We find solace in the knowledge that Heaven awaits us, and one day, we will be reunited with our loved ones. Even in moments of sorrow, we can still experience joy. Followers of Christ receive comfort and assurance from the promises and word of our God. He has called us His friends. Everything in our lives, whether large or small, works toward a significant, meaningful, and intended outcome. The writer tells us in Isaiah 57:2, *"Those who walk uprightly enter into peace; they find rest as they lie in death."* Hoping in Christ, we can find peace and rest even during grief and tragedy.

Many individuals link their identity, self-worth, and value to their careers, marriages, children, or material possessions. When these aspects stumble, and relationships deteriorate, people often question their faith, God's will, purpose, and power. Some might even turn away from the Christian life, while others may completely abandon their belief in God. These reactions often reveal a flawed understanding of and relationship with God. Many identify as Christians by name without genuinely committing to follow Christ. They frequently overlook that God controls everything, even in times of chaos. Because He is in control, the faithful hold on to Him.

True faith requires surrendering control and trusting in God's perfect plan. By practicing genuine faith, we profoundly draw closer to God and experience His presence. Developing trust can be challenging without a relationship with God, so studying His Word, reflecting, praying, and worshiping is essential. Scripture teaches that faith comes from hearing the Word, so we should not neglect attending church and engaging in communal fellowship. Regularly surrounding ourselves with fellow believers strengthens our commitment, dedication, and resolve along this faith journey.

God has a tremendous and meaningful purpose for each of our unique lives. Regardless of our challenges, we can pray through every experience and witness the goodness of God. Difficulties serve as opportunities to strengthen our personal and intimate relationship with Him. As stated in Nahum 1:7, "The Lord is good, a strong refuge when trouble comes. He is close to those who trust in him." Even when His presence feels distant, seek His footprints in the sand—He is always carrying us. Invite Him to take complete control of your life and allow Him to be glorified in every area. During testing, hold onto the assurance that His will for you is good, pleasing, and perfect. He never asks us to strive to understand everything. On the contrary, He asks us only to trust Him.

## Prayer:

Father, thank you for your words, which remind us that we can fully trust you to meet our needs in every season of life. Lord, I pray that whoever reads this book will recognize the importance of having a relationship with you. I pray their souls will long for you, and their roots will grow deep as they diligently seek you. Please help those struggling with life's challenges and the many transitions we face. In Jesus' mighty name, I pray. Amen.

## Meditating Scriptures:

**Matthew 5:4** – "Blessed are those who mourn, for they shall be comforted."

### Key Points and Reminders

- Completely surrender to the plan and will of God
- Seek God and ask Him to fill every part of you until there is no space
- Remember, there is no pain that God is not aware of and will not heal

# Reflection

No relationship can be one-sided. Building, fostering, and maintaining a strong and productive relationship requires the participation and effort of everyone involved. Without this, there can be no familiarity, connection, or closeness.

# DAY 24
# GOD IN UNCERTAIN TIMES

**Psalm 34:17** – "When the righteous cry for help, the LORD hears and delivers them out of all their troubles."

You are mistaken if you think you're blessed solely by material possessions and wealth. Each day, God grants us marvelous gifts that no amount of money can buy, such as waking up with breath and a beating heart, using your limbs, and being able to experience and embrace new opportunities. These are testaments to God's grace, which we often take for granted. This truth reminds us that we are genuinely blessed and favored in profound ways we may not always acknowledge.

No matter the situation, God will support and guide you. In both good times and challenges, you are never alone. He stands by you during loss, depression, anxiety, job struggles, or feelings of isolation, providing comfort and preparing you for what's next. God uses struggles to strengthen our faith and build our spiritual resilience. As His ambassadors, He calls us to maintain unwavering faith, as it can move mountains. If our faith is in Christ, we can find comfort in God and confidently proclaim, as the writer states in Hebrews 13:6, "*So we can say with confidence, The Lord is my helper, so I will not fear.*"

The journey of spiritual growth is often challenging and devoid of glamour. It is filled with hardships, tears, and confusion. During tough times, we may struggle to understand God's intentions or His silence. While questioning our challenges, we often forget that God rarely reveals His plan immediately. On the contrary, He asks us to trust Him, as He knows the end from the beginning. No matter the circumstance, we can find comfort in knowing God is with us through every situation. In the storms, God is always present.

Experiencing moments of uncertainty is inevitable. However, it's important to remember that our human emotions do not influence God during these times. Despite feelings and emotions, He asks us to trust Him. God is moved by faith, not by our feelings. As followers of Christ, we are reminded in 2 Corinthians 5:7 that we must "walk by faith, not by sight." We don't need to understand the details of God's plans. On the contrary, we need faith to confidently believe that God is omniscient (knowing everything) and sovereign (ruler of the world). God knows what He's doing, and we can trust Him.

I recognize that I am not a perfect Christian and may not conform to traditional ideals. However, who truly fulfills such expectations? In times of struggle and challenge, wrestling with the idea of God's sovereignty is natural. While we often aim to avoid discomfort, pain, and hardship, growth frequently occurs beyond our comfort zones. Spiritual development involves trusting God's faithfulness, even in fear and uncertainty. Lamentations 3:32 beautifully expresses, "Though he brings grief, he also shows compassion because of the greatness of his unfailing love."

As mature Christians, we must recognize and accept that God governs our lives and that facing challenges is an inherent part of our journey. The author of Job 14:1-2 poignantly illustrates the fragility of human existence, lamenting, "How short is life, how full of trouble! We bloom like flowers and then fade away. Like a fleeting shadow, we quickly vanish." Even when we acknowledge this truth, we still experience moments of frustration, during which Satan attempts to manipulate our emotions with deception and false narratives. Lucifer, the father of lies, cannot convey the truth. We must rise above thoughts of fear, worry, and doubt, as these do not come from God, who grants us a spirit of courage. As James 4:7-8 encourages us, "Humble yourselves before God, resist the devil, and he will flee from you. Draw near to God, and He will draw near to you."

Praise and worship music can profoundly impact the soul during times of challenge and struggle, fostering a deep connection with God. The intentional habit and practice of praise and worship can be an antidote to the pains we experience during life's most enduring challenges. When anchored in Christ, the situation or outcomes matter less when God is glorified. God is not a genie to fulfill our desires; He is our sovereign Lord and Creator. We are like clay in the hands of a Potter, to be shaped as He sees fit. Having faith and trust in His immeasurable wisdom gives us confidence that He knows what is best for us. Acknowledging our weaknesses leads us to a more profound yearning for His presence and the eternal home prepared through Christ Jesus.

# Prayer:

I pray that God grants you wisdom to understand His will for your life. May He help you examine your motives, ambitions, and the purpose of your prayers and deepen your spiritual growth. May all your requests come from a sincere desire to please God. May God strengthen your weaknesses and bless you with unwavering trust in Him. I pray that you will seek God fervently and walk closely with Him each day. May God answer your prayers and grant you peace, in Jesus' name. Amen.

# Meditating Scriptures:

**Isaiah 43:2** – "When you pass through the waters, I will be with you; and through the rivers, they shall not overwhelm you; when you walk through the fire you shall not be burned, and the flame shall not consume you."

### Key Points and Reminders

- Remember, God is always in charge
- Trust and have faith
- Trust in God's timing and process

# Reflection

Some yearn for the fleeting treasures of this world: silver, diamonds, emeralds, and gold. Acknowledging the worthlessness of these temporary possessions, the wise long for and fervently pursue Christ Jesus, the shepherd of weary and sick souls.

# DAY 25
# THE STRUGGLE AND BATTLE OF BEING A CHRISTIAN

**Galatians 5:24**: "Those who belong to Christ Jesus have nailed the passions and desires of their sinful nature to his cross and crucified them there."

Christians embark on a profound internal spiritual journey where opposing forces vie for our attention. Each day offers the chance to balance the desires of the flesh with the guidance of the spirit, as each seeks different outcomes. This ongoing struggle between our physical urges and upholding spiritual principles is challenging and transformative. Our natural inclination is to gravitate toward what seems appealing and fulfilling. However, as the apostle Paul reminds us in Galatians 5:17-18, a significant conflict arises, as the sinful nature yearns for what opposes the spirit's intentions. Despite this tension, we possess the incredible gift of free will. Living a life that reflects the spirit requires intentional effort and dedication, and this commitment drives us forward on our spiritual journey.

Humans are prone to failure when relying solely on physical strength and abilities. Without the guidance and support of the Holy Spirit, we remain governed by our ideas, feelings, emotions, desires, and passions. In his message to the Galatians, the Apostle Paul warns that those who pursue their desires exhibit behaviors such as sexual immorality, impurity, idolatry, hostility, jealousy, and selfish ambition (Galatians 5:19-21). He emphasizes that such individuals will not inherit the Kingdom of God. The Scripture is clear and unapologetic. You can recognize if they belong to Christ by examining their fruit.

As children of God, we are people of the Book, with His Word serving as our ultimate authority and guide. Living according to His Word is essential to fulfilling God's plan. While it may not always be easy, we should seek the power of God, which is always available if we ask, empowering us to endure any trials that come our way. In Matthew 7:9-11, the Lord Jesus provided an analogy, asking if fathers would give their children something harmful if they asked for something good. Of course not! Similarly, if even sinful people know how to give good gifts to their children, how much more will our heavenly Father give the Holy Spirit to those who ask Him?

While many read Scripture, its teachings, precepts, and principles are often not applied. Some churchgoers behave like non-believers, making it challenging for outsiders to grasp what being a Christian truly signifies and means. As followers of Christ, we are called to a higher standard and should strive to reflect our commitment to Him, demonstrating the essence of our faith to those seeking understanding. We are reminded in Galatians 5:22-23 that "the Holy Spirit produces this kind of fruit in the lives of followers of Christ: love, joy, peace, patience, kindness, goodness, faithfulness, gentleness, and self-control. There is no law against these things!" Let's consciously choose to be led by the Holy Spirit and live a life that shows His love, goodness, and unmistakable transformative power!

# Prayer:

As a fellow servant of Christ, I pray that the word of God nourishes your soul and that the love of God inspires you to live following His Kingdom agenda. My prayer is that you shine as a light in every room you enter and that the anointing of God increases upon you daily. May your face radiate like the sun so the world knows and recognizes you as a follower of The Way, a Born-Again Believer. I ask these things in the Mighty Name of Jesus, Amen!

# Meditating Scriptures:

**Proverbs 3:5- 6** – "Trust in the Lord with all your heart and lean not on your own understanding. In all your ways, submit to him; he will make your paths straight."

**John 16:33** – "I have told you these things, so that you may have peace in me. In this world, you may have trouble. But take heart! I have overcome the world."

## Key Points and Reminders

- Die a little more each day to lust, desires, and passions
- Let prayer be as natural as breathing
- Strive to bring light wherever there is darkness

## Reflection

There is immense comfort in knowing that even when everything seems lost and nothing supports you, Jehovah-Jireh, the Great Provider, is always there.

## DAY 26
# MORE OF JESUS AND LESS OF THE WORLD

**John 17:15-21:** Jesus Prayer: "My prayer is not that you take them out of the world but that you protect them from the evil one. They are not of the world, even as I am not of it. Sanctify them by the truth; your word is truth. As you sent me into the world, I have sent them into the world. My prayer is not for them alone. I pray also for those who will believe in me through their message, that all of them may be one, Father, just as you are in me, and I am in you. May they also be in us so the world may believe you have sent me".

As a Christian, my goal is to reach heaven. In the meantime, however, I deeply desire to please the Lord with how I spend my time on earth. Pleasing the Lord should be the most critical objective for all Christians. After all, we are His children, and we should strive with determination to bring honor and glory to His name. As Ecclesiastes 12:13 states, we must fear God and obey His commands. Therefore, we should seek to please the Father with diligence and enthusiasm.

The writer of Hebrews 11:6 says that it's "impossible to please God without faith. To come to Him, we must believe He exists and (rewards) those who seek Him sincerely." This faith is not a distant concept but a living reality that we can experience through hearing the Good News about Christ, as stated in Romans 10:17. The key to change is allowing the power and integrity of the Bible to minister to our hearts. Transformation and knowing God is an inside job. Knowing God starts internally with the circumcision of the heart. Only then can renewal and regeneration begin, making us more and more like Christ Jesus each day.

Devoting time to reading and meditating on God's word brings about joyful transformation as we draw nearer to Him. As the wax melts before the fire, our character shifts in His presence, enabling us to reflect His nature. Each encounter with God's power ignites a more profound longing for Him. Psalm 34:8 invites us to "taste and see that the Lord is good. Blessed is the one who takes refuge in him."

Physical hunger and spiritual hunger are different. While physical hunger can feel insatiable, spiritual hunger finds satisfaction in Christ, as fulfillment comes from God. If your desire for God and His presence diminishes, see this as an opportunity to start fresh and renew your relationship with Him. A lack of longing may indicate a gradual drifting away. By intentionally seeking a connection with God, you can realign yourself and deepen your spiritual connection, experiencing His presence and the power of His Spirit more profoundly and meaningfully.

God desires that we fully and completely give ourselves to Him, allowing ourselves to be consumed by His Spirit. The Apostle Paul urges us in Romans 12:1-2 to "offer our bodies as a living sacrifice, holy and pleasing to God, which is our true and proper worship." He also advises us not to conform to this world's patterns, practices, and behaviors but to be transformed by renewing our minds so we can test and prove what God's good, pleasing, and perfect will is.

Here are a few questions:

What kind of Christian do you aspire to be? Reflect on your level of passion—are you actively engaged in your faith, or is there room for growth? Consider whether you gravitate more toward spiritual pursuits or worldly concerns. Are you fully committed to your beliefs, or do you occasionally hesitate? How deeply do you long for God's word, and how consistently are you seeking a closer relationship with Him? This introspection can guide your spiritual journey and help nurture a more vibrant faith.

God is accessible to anyone pursuing a genuine relationship with Him. He hears our sincere requests, even when He may seem silent. We should remain hopeful, for He is loving and compassionate. His silence teaches us patience and perseverance in prayer. Matthew 7:7 encourages us to keep asking and seeking; the doors will open in time. We can learn more about Him by focusing on His words and praying earnestly. God desires a close relationship with us, so let's continue to seek Him through prayer and study. Our persistence fosters hope and encouragement while building a stronger and closer relationship and connection with Him.

# Prayer:

Heavenly Father, thank You for overcoming temptation. You are a perfect example of holiness. Please strengthen me in my weaknesses and be my foundation. Help me keep earthly achievements in perspective and always give You glory. May I continually praise You for all You do in my life. In the Mighty Name of Jesus, I pray, Amen!

# Meditating Scriptures:

**James 4:7** – "**S**ubmit yourselves therefore to God. Resist the devil, and he will flee from you."

**Hebrews 4:15** – "**For** we do not have a high priest who cannot sympathize with our weaknesses, but one who has been tempted in all things as we are, yet without sin."

## Key Points and Reminders

- Allow the Word of God to transform you
- Embrace the teachings and truths of the scriptures and be ready to experience their power
- Desire the power and presence of Christ in your life above all else

# Reflection

Success is never a result of chance, accident, or coincidence. Instead, it demands intentionality and practical and spiritual growth in all areas of life.

# DAY 27
# LIFE CAN BE TOUGH!

**2 Corinthians 12:9** - "My grace is all you need. My power works best in weakness." So now I am glad to boast about my weaknesses so that the power of Christ can work through me.

---

Sometimes, life can feel overwhelming, filled with fears, heartaches, and sorrows. Each day, we face challenges that can significantly impact our lives. It's natural to feel distressed when we witness or endure difficult struggles, whether public or private. As Christians, we are not exempt from these feelings. However, amidst trials, suffering, and hardships, we can find comfort and hope in John 16:33: "In this world, you will have trouble. But take heart! I have overcome the world." This reminder encourages us not to give up, even when life feels unbearable.

During challenging times, we must acknowledge our pain and need for support and support one another. As followers of Christ, building a community gives us the comfort of fellow laborers who help support and uplift those in need. We remind each other that Christ is our strength and that He has overcome the world. In moments of distress, turmoil, and anguish, this bond is a powerful source of healing. In times of despair, let us hold firmly to the truth that God is always with us and shows compassion for our circumstances, encouraging us to exhibit greater empathy toward ourselves and those around us. We are not alone in facing life's challenges; we can find renewed strength and hope together by supporting one another.

People set various personal goals and resolutions at the beginning of each year. Initially, everyone is filled with hope and the promise of a fresh start. However, life can be unpredictable. Unexpected events can suddenly disrupt our carefully crafted plans, leaving us discouraged, disappointed, and deeply troubled. In these moments, holding onto our hope and faith is crucial. During times of frustration and uncertainty, we must remember that God is with us; even when we cannot see Him, feel Him, or grasp His plan, He still guides us through life's unpredictability. This realization can be a tremendous source of encouragement and tranquility.

When life doesn't progress in the direction we desire or at a different pace than we expected, we have a choice. We can give in to fleeting emotions, fears, and anxieties, or we can stand firm on the promises of God's word and continue moving forward. Regardless of the situation or circumstances, we must remain optimistic, encouraged, confident, and assured that God has good plans for our future. We can take comfort in the words of Jeremiah 29:11, "I know the plans I have for you," declares the Lord, "plans to prosper you and not to harm you, plans to give you hope and a future." These plans serve as a beacon of hope, reminding us that our future is in God's hands, filled with promise and possibility.

## **The story**

As I finished graduate school and was about to embark on a new career, alongside the excitement of celebrating my tenth wedding anniversary, I couldn't shake a sense of unease. No matter how much I prayed and sought the Lord, this feeling wouldn't disappear. This sense lingered despite my time in the Word, consistent prayer, and regular spiritual discipline.

As my birthday approached, I longed for days filled with relaxation, fun, beautiful surroundings, and a break from the monotony of daily life. In His kindness, God answered my prayers and exceeded my expectations. My husband and I enjoyed sixteen glorious days in Southeast Asia to celebrate my birthday. This trip was everything I needed and more. Although we have traveled to many countries, this journey was among the most relaxing, enjoyable, and memorable. Each day began with warm weather and a delightful breakfast. I savored long, leisurely walks on pristine beaches, fantastic street food, and vibrant night markets. However, these moments of bliss would soon be interrupted.

Before returning from my trip, I received some disturbing news: my niece had been taken to the hospital. Her mother, my older sister, had assaulted her. This news upset me greatly and left me at a loss for words. However, despite being deeply troubled, I was not entirely shocked, as my family has a history of dramatic and troubling situations. My sister has a pattern of manic episodes, anger, and violence. Although profoundly saddened, I managed to maintain a sense of inner peace and contentment, refusing to let this event steal the joy and peace that the Lord had granted me during my time away.

After returning home, the enemy's attacks began one after another. Seemingly endless family concerns and issues started to weigh on me. Each week brought a new problem that appeared out of nowhere. Nevertheless, amid a barrage of satanic assaults and spiritual attacks, I continually sought the Lord in prayer for help and strength. Despite it all, He remained a steadfast friend, my rock, unfailing refuge, and the source of support in times of trouble.

As graduation approached, I found it hard to maintain my excitement. A week before commencement, I received a distressing call about my mother. To my surprise, at fifty-nine, she had been diagnosed with a rare form of dementia. Before her diagnosis, I had no reason to suspect or believe she was sick or mentally declining at all. Initially, I perceived the changes as symptoms of tiredness or depression. However, after some time and conversations with her on the phone, my initial hopes were dashed, and I realized something was wrong and that she needed medical attention.

When I returned home, my worst fears were confirmed. My mother's mental abilities had deteriorated drastically. I was shocked and heartbroken. Despite suffering in silence, I felt obliged to appear brave and unaffected for her sake. It has been challenging to witness someone who has always been a symbol of strength, capability, and resilience now in a childlike state, unable to recognize simple objects, colors, and letters or think clearly and reason. Often, when I'm alone, my heart breaks. It's daunting to no longer have the mother I once knew so well. However, the Great Counselor reminds me of His grace. He has remained my source of contentment and peace, consistently providing everything I need as I navigate this unforeseen journey.

As Christians, we are not exempt from life's hardships. The writer of Job 14:1-2 reflects on this truth, saying, "How frail is humanity! How short life is, how full of trouble! We blossom like flowers and then wither. Like a passing shadow, we quickly disappear."

Shortly after coming to terms with my mother's condition, I faced even greater devastation. My little brother's longtime friend and my ex-boyfriend of seven years, whom I have known since third grade, were tragically killed within two weeks of each other. Though I was deeply shaken by these events, my faith and hope in God remained strong. I found comfort in Psalm 34:18: "*The Lord is close to the brokenhearted and saves those who are crushed in spirit.*"

Amid these challenges and trials, prayer became essential. The habit and practice of praying without ceasing grew more necessary. Prayer not only allowed me to present my concerns, anxieties, fears, and petitions to God, but it also proved therapeutic. This intense and focused prayer time enhanced my concentration and magnified my confidence in the Lord's ability and power to heal the brokenhearted. These hardships taught me that the Lord can and will reveal Himself as mighty and strong during heartache and pain. The key is to believe that He can, and with certainty, He will in due time!

God provides strength and comfort to His children. Focusing on problems or circumstances will not change them; we should focus on God's promises. I experience moments of sadness and tears, yet I find solace in knowing that God is a healer who lifts those who are downcast. Even during difficult times, I am reminded of Jesus' words in Matthew 11:28: "*Come to me, all you who are weary and burdened, and I will give you rest.*"

Life presents many challenges, but we can always rely on our faithful and unfailing Lord. He keeps His promises to those who trust Him. Sin introduced pain into the world, making suffering and hardships a part of the human experience. However, for those who place their hope in God, we are never alone. The Lord assures us in Hebrews 13:5-6, "I will never fail you. I will never abandon you." Because of this truth, we can confidently declare, like David, "*The Lord is my helper; I will not fear.*"

Regardless of the situation or circumstance, the Lord our God is with us, ready to help whenever we call.

## Prayer:

Father, I thank you for always being a present help in times of trouble. Thank you for comforting us in calamity and distress and for your peace that surpasses human understanding. I pray for those who are in agony from life's pain. Strengthen and heal them and allow them to experience your presence in their need. Please meet every need and help them to depend on you daily. In Jesus' name, Amen!

## Meditating Scriptures:

**Psalm 23:4** – "Even when I walk through the darkest valley, I will not be afraid, for you are close beside me. Your rod and your staff protect and comfort me."

### Key Points and Reminders

- Don't expect your journey to be easy. Jesus never claimed it would be
- Trust in God's plan and purpose for your life
- We are never alone; God is always there to help us

**Reflection**

There are distractions everywhere. Everything is changing rapidly, morphing, and moving too fast. The lights and sounds are designed to be alluring. However, those who call on the name of the Lord must keep their focus firmly on Christ Jesus. We cannot afford to lose focus. Our minds and gaze must remain constantly on Him.

# DAY 28
# REJOICE. BELIEVERS WILL NEVER DIE!

**1 Corinthians 15:22** – "Just as everyone dies because we belong to Adam, everyone who belongs to Christ will be given new life."

Do you often reflect on what lies beyond this life and the concept of immortality? I do, and it sparks deep contemplation. What will it feel like to say goodbye to this reality? These questions can be troubling or frightening for many. However, for those with faith in Christ, this perspective shifts. Believers find confidence in their future and destiny, and the fear dissipates when they know where they will spend eternity.

As a believer in Christ Jesus, I find comfort in the promise that our mortal bodies will one day be transformed, free from decay and death. This assurance strengthens believers everywhere. In 1 Corinthians 15:42-44, the Apostle Paul explains that our earthly bodies will be raised in glory and power, transformed into immortal bodies free from world limitations. The transformation from mortality to immortality is a source of hope for believers. Scriptures affirm, "Our earthly bodies are buried in brokenness and weakness, but they will be raised in glory and strength as spiritual bodies."

Because we are united with Christ, we can look forward to becoming like Him one day! His triumph over death means we, too, will experience new life. This incredible promise is available to everyone who believes. While sin can lead us down a difficult path, God lovingly offers us eternal life through Christ Jesus. When we accept Him, we receive peace and hope. However, turning away from God means missing out on the transition to Heaven. Remember the words of John 3:36: "Whoever believes in the Son has eternal life, but whoever rejects the Son will not see life, for God's wrath remains on them." It's all about embracing and receiving that wonderful gift!

As believers in God, our hope is anchored in Christ's glorious return. We are anxious in anticipation of the beautiful home He has prepared. We look forward to heavenly treasures and rewards, including the crown of rejoicing, where God will wipe away every tear. There will be no more death or sorrow (Revelation 21:4). The Crown of Righteousness awaits those who love the Lord (2 Timothy 4:8), while the Crown of Life is for those who endure suffering for our Savior Christ Jesus (Revelation 2:10). The Crown of Glory is for all who long for His appearance (1 Peter 5:4). With joyful hearts, we will behold God!

I find immense joy in knowing that the Creator of the universe is mindful of us and has prepared a place in His kingdom. This truth offers comfort and stirs anticipation. While you may not own a house on earth, an eternal home awaits in heaven, crafted by God, untouched by decay. This promise is for the children of the Great King. As 1 Corinthians 15:54-55 reminds us, "When our dying bodies are transformed, death is swallowed up in victory."

Though we cannot escape the decay of our mortal bodies and will eventually fall asleep, we will never truly die! The Lord's words are always true. As stated in 2 Corinthians 5:4, "While we live in these earthly bodies, we groan and sigh... Rather, we long to put on our new bodies so that these dying bodies will be swallowed up by life."

No matter what the present holds, I encourage you to reflect on heaven's reality and eternity's certainty. Believers have the promise of salvation and eternal life, while non-believers face spiritual separation. We all must choose between life and death. Christ Jesus is the way to everlasting life, offering hope to everyone, regardless of their past. This is an invitation to embrace hope and build a relationship with Him.

# Prayer:

Father, thank you for preparing a place for your children in your Kingdom and assuring us of salvation beyond this life. Please help us to let go of the temporary things in this world and invest in the treasures that await us in heaven. Ignite within us an unwavering focus on your Heavenly Kingdom in our hearts, our true home. Keep our hearts and minds focused as we stand firmly in that hope, eagerly awaiting your glorious return. In Jesus' name, I pray. Amen.

# Meditating Scriptures

**1 Corinthians 15:58** – "So, my dear brothers and sisters, be strong and immovable. Always work enthusiastically for the Lord; you know that nothing you do for the Lord is ever useless."

## Key Points and Reminders

- Rejoice in the fact that you will live again
- Concentrate on eternity
- Find solace in God's promises

# Reflection

If we lose everything—money, family, and friends—and face life's greatest calamities with peace nowhere to be found, our God, Jehovah-Rophe, the Lord Who Heals, remains faithful and worthy of our unwavering adoration and praise.

# DAY 29
# HIGHLIGHT THE GOODNESS OF GOD

**Ephesians 5:19-21 –** "Sing and make music from your heart to the Lord, always giving thanks to God the Father for everything, in the name of our Lord Jesus Christ."

How often do you reflect on God's goodness and express gratitude? How frequently do you consider what He has done in your life that brings you indescribable joy? I've learned the importance of being thankful for everything, including disappointments. Finding the silver lining in every situation has transformed my attitude and deepened my understanding of the Lord and His sovereignty.

Through the Holy Spirit, God has blessed me with a renewed perspective. My prayer life is now a continuous act of thanksgiving and praise, honoring God's wisdom and plans for me. I've learned to maintain gratitude and praise regardless of my circumstances.

The Lord has taught me to start every prayer with gratitude, recognizing that He owes me nothing and has given me more than I can repay. Reflecting on His kindness motivates me to offer the praise He deserves. Because of His boundless favor, I focus on His goodness rather than circumstances beyond my control.

I recognize God's guiding hand in my life. He has shown me incredible goodness, and I have felt His presence in many situations. His miraculous protection has taught me to remain grateful through trials. No matter what happens, He deserves praise, and I will bless the Lord.

As one of His dear children, I embrace everything He allows, trusting that it all works together for my good. I find comfort in His faithfulness and unwavering presence, whether in joy or sorrow. God provides protection and grace, inspiring me to lift my voice in praise. I am grateful for all He has done, as it is written in 1 Thessalonians 5:18: "Give thanks in all circumstances; for this is the will of God in Christ Jesus for you."

I've faced many challenges that tested my faith and resolve throughout my journey. I've navigated dark and deep valleys and struggled to find the motivation to pray, feeling the weight of responsibilities in family, work, and friendships. Yet, I've never been alone; God's favor has guided me through difficult moments. Because of this, I am grateful and inspired to continue praising Him.

When facing challenges, I've learned that praising God allows me to release my worries and trust in His control. I'm grateful that He cares for us. Psalm 95:2 reminds us: "Let us come into His presence with thanksgiving; let us make a joyful noise to Him with songs of praise!"

Living in gratitude transforms our focus from circumstances to God. When God is our focal point, we find the strength to face difficulties and challenges and glorify Him. His will is perfect, often exceeding our expectations, even when His plans remain unclear. As David states in Psalm 34:1-3, "I will praise the Lord at all times… Let us proclaim the Lord's greatness."

Since becoming a believer in the Lord Jesus Christ, I've shared my testimony about God's amazing grace with people from diverse backgrounds. Each time I express His love—how He saved and transformed me—I experience immense joy. Testifying about the Savior's grace and reflecting on His work fills my heart with worship and gratitude, especially during challenging times.

Recognizing our limitations and unworthiness of His love inspires gratitude. Despite not deserving it, He graciously offers countless blessings, including jobs, homes, and health. Most importantly, He demonstrated profound love by sacrificing Himself for our sins. He continually provides us with reconciliation and redemption. Considering His immeasurable love and grace, we should respond with reverence, gratitude, and praise—Hallelujah! Acknowledging His goodness should encourage continuous appreciation and thankfulness as we reflect on His favor.

# Prayer:

Father, I thank You for Your ability and power to change hearts. Thank You for all that You have done and continue to do. Bless us, inspire us, and teach us to give You all the honor, glory, and praise alone. In Jesus' name, Amen.

# Meditating Scriptures

**Colossians 3:15** – "Let the peace of Christ rule in your hearts, since as members of one body you were called to peace. And be thankful."

## Key Points and Reminders

- Focus on God's goodness
- Trust God's guidance and direction
- Stay grateful

# Reflection

We often debate who is qualified to serve God in various roles. Unfortunately, we frequently judge based on outward appearances. Yet, God evaluates people according to their hearts, not their qualifications. Unlike humans, Jehovah Sabaoth, the Lord of Hosts, chooses those with the right heart who are willing, prepared, and available.

# DAY 30
# WILLING, WAITING, AND AVAILABLE

**Psalms 27:14**- "Wait for the Lord; be strong and take heart and wait for the Lord."

Honestly, I never considered myself a writer, nor did I ever imagine I would write a book. This book results from the encouragement and support from my husband and one of my closest friends. They both nudged and urged me, and I believe God guided them to push me forward. Despite my fears and doubts, I was willing, open, and available. Through this experience, along with countless others, I have learned that God does not show favoritism and remains faithful even to those who are unfaithful. I also understand that God is not concerned with our excuses for what we can or cannot do. He is ready to use anyone willing and open to His guidance, including those who may not seem capable or talented but are prepared to be available.

2019, I strongly desired to draw closer to God and strengthen my spiritual commitment. In my daily prayers, I asked God to speak to me and help me feel His presence more profoundly and frequently. One morning, I woke up early and sat quietly, eagerly anticipating a message from the Lord. My heart was open and ready to receive any guidance, whether big or small. Each day, I developed a routine of rising early, finding a quiet spot, and praying, yearning to hear the voice of the Lord. Mornings became my sacred time to connect with God, even amidst His silence. I believe profound peace awaits in His presence, regardless of whether He chooses to speak. Reflecting on the Lord's goodness, David proclaimed in Psalms 16:11, *"You will show me the way of life, granting me the joy of Your presence and the pleasures of living with You forever."*

One day, while reading the scriptures, the Holy Spirit prompted me to share my thoughts on social media. Following this guidance, I regularly posted my daily scripture readings and devotions that resonated deeply with my soul. Before posting, I often discussed my reflections with my husband. Over time, after noticing the positive impact of my posts, my husband suggested, "You should write a book." His idea surprised me; it was both encouraging and somewhat daunting. Initially, I felt inadequate and uncertain because my husband is an exceptional academic and scholar. He is an overachiever—intelligent, creative, and talented in many areas. Moreover, he is a pastor, theologian, outstanding speaker, and gifted writer who has authored several books. Calling him an overachiever is truly an understatement, as he has earned not one but two doctoral degrees by God's grace.

Still uncertain, my husband encouraged me to share my feelings with a close friend. After discussing my doubts, apprehensions, and fears with her, she confirmed my husband's perspective that I should pursue writing a book. Unlike them, I could never have imagined anything I thought or wrote could be significant enough to be published. However, my friend Shona emphasized the importance of leaving a record and testimony for future generations. Respecting the opinions and wisdom of my husband and friend—both outstanding teachers and preachers of God's Word, as well as fellow Christians—along with external confirmation, I felt compelled to start writing. Although I still felt insecure and intimidated, I reflected on the words of Proverbs 13:20, which states, *"Whoever walks with the wise becomes wise, but the companion of fools will suffer harm."*

Before writing this book, the Lord strongly affirmed its necessity, potential impact, and significance. Every post I shared received encouraging feedback, with many expressing gratitude for my courage and faith. I was also requested to continue sharing and increase the frequency of my posts. While this outpouring of support has been truly uplifting, early on, it became clear that many viewers might not engage beyond simply reading the posts without leaving a like or a comment. However, validation and acknowledgment have never motivated me to post.

From the beginning, my motivation has been driven by the prompting of the Holy Spirit. Early on this journey, the Holy Spirit communicated with me, clearly stating that someone is always watching and being influenced by my posts and how I showcase my life, whether they comment or not. He spoke to me directly, emphasizing that my motivation and validation should never arise from seeking likes or comments. God calls me to remain obedient, willing, and available regardless of likes, comments, or dislikes.

The purpose of writing this book is to share the gospel of the Lord Jesus Christ and provide testimony about everything the Lord has done in my life. My heartfelt prayer is that my obedience, despite my doubts, apprehensions, and fears surrounding this labor of love, will encourage, inspire, and motivate readers to develop a deeper relationship with the Lord and draw closer to Him. The Lord shows no favoritism and has promised that anyone who comes to Him will never be rejected or cast aside. If He can save someone like me and completely transform my life, He can do the same for anyone who sincerely seeks Him and desires to know Him more intimately.

As I mentioned earlier, I have never seen myself as a writer. It took me several years to finish this book. From the beginning, I found it almost impossible to write a single word unless God placed it in my spirit. Everything that has made its way onto the page is what God has breathed and inspired. We are reminded in John 7:38, "Whoever believes in me, as the Scripture has said, out of his or her heart will flow rivers of living water." Please understand, dear reader, that I am nothing without the Lord. It is only through Him that I can accomplish anything. Because of this truth, I must give all glory and honor to Him, and I encourage you to do the same.

I may not know who will read this book, but I am committed to the work that the Father has called me to do. As someone named by Christ, I must fulfill the Great Commission and share the message of my wonderful Savior with the world. In Matthew 28:19, Jesus commands His disciples to spread His message, saying, "Go and make disciples of all nations." I have made myself available for Him to use, and I am striving to share His message and inspire every reader of this book. Your reading this book is not by chance; it is the Lord's will for you to know Him intimately, authentically, and deeply.

Beloved, if you wish to be used by God, lay everything at His feet.

He has given us all (something) we can use to win souls for His kingdom. As followers of Christ, children of the Great King, we should live with a singular goal, purpose, and objective—to serve God in every way we can. God is not concerned with our excuses; He desires us to be willing, waiting, and available so that when He calls, we can respond, "Here I am. I am available; send me."

# Prayer:

Father, I pray that You will be gracious and kind. Speak to the hearts and minds of all who read these words. Please help them to be patient, courageous, willing, and available to be used by You in any way that brings You glory and honor. In Jesus' name. Amen.

# Meditating Scriptures:

**Matthew 28:19-20-** "Therefore go and make disciples of all the nations, baptizing them in the name of the Father and the Son and the Holy Spirit. [20] Teach these new disciples to obey all the commands I have given you. And be sure I am with you always, even to the end of the age."

## Key Points and Reminders

- Remain open, ready, and available for God's use and service
- Draw near to God to nurture trust and commitment
- Trust God throughout the process and for the outcome

# Reflection

Made in the USA
Middletown, DE
17 September 2025